# Praise for *Tues*

"This book hits all the marks, and it goes straight to the heart. Tina Welling beautifully captures the humanity of the inmates, and reminds us, through gorgeously written prose, that we are all so much more alike than we are different and that deep down we all long to be seen, heard, and loved. I hope everyone reads this captivating book."

— **Tiffanie DeBartolo**, author of *SORROW*, *God-Shaped Hole*, and *How to Kill a Rockstar*

"As much of a page-turner as *Tuesdays with Morrie*, *Tuesdays in Jail* opens locked doors and liberates creativity, compassion, and unexpected community. Tina Welling's book is a gift of rare vistas elegantly shared. Unquestionably a must-read for this year."

— **William Powers**, author of *Twelve by Twelve: A One-Room Cabin Off the Grid and Beyond the American Dream*

"*Tuesdays in Jail* is a lesson in living. Tina Welling's writing skillfully illuminates the intricacies of those whose narratives we don't often hear. Writing with empathy and open-mindedness, Welling takes us on an uplifting journey as she tells us her own story. This memoir of sorts is an important testament to those society forgets and to the power of storytelling. A heart-rending read, this book is a sensitive exploration of the journeys we take, with practical lessons embedded in the text."

— **Nina McConigley**, author of *Cowboys and East Indians*, PEN Open Book Award winner

"Tina Welling writes an empathetic, lyrical testament. Countless Tuesdays, she went into the Teton County Detention Center in Wyoming to help male inmates find their souls through writing in drugstore journals with number 2 pencils. Her crisp sentences honor inmates with long penal sentences of their own. This is memoir and manual. Through writing, drunks and addicts and thieves and batterers unlock trapped feelings. A baptism in hope and possibility, this book confirms what I have long thought: creativity saves us."

— **Spencer Reece**, author of *The Clerk's Tale* and *The Road to Emmaus*, long-listed for the National Book Award

"Throughout this book, Tina Welling shares her wisdom and insight into teaching writing skills to those who are incarcerated. Through her examples of dialogue, lessons, and conversations, she brings out the creativity and potential in those who have been often overlooked in our society, proving that these individuals do have a voice and should be given the opportunity to be educated, included, and heard."

— **Vita Pires**, executive director of the Prison Mindfulness Institute

"On rare occasions you read a book by a person who is not only a fine writer but also a natural wizard of empathy. Some people say, 'I feel so strongly I can't put it into words.' Tina Welling can put it into words. She articulates the deepest of emotions, both her own and those of the prisoners she works with. She understands what she feels, and then she goes on to understand what the prisoners feel. Read *Tuesdays in Jail*."

— **Tim Sandlin**, author of the *GroVont* series of novels

"In *Tuesdays in Jail*, Tina Welling illuminates the inherent dignity of a human life. She explores, through striking and self-revealing prose, how each of us can connect to our personal power and sense of aliveness. This book is a profound reminder of our shared humanity."

— **Katherine Standefer**, author of *Lightning Flowers*

"Read *Tuesdays in Jail* and accompany Tina Welling on visits to a place people rarely experience. Sit in on intimate and inspiring discussions not often associated with the incarcerated. As Welling says, 'The inmates and I had a lot of characteristics in common. It's just that they had been arrested and I had not.'"

— **John Travis**, guiding teacher at Mountain Stream Meditation

# Tuesdays in Jail

## Also by Tina Welling

**Nonfiction**

*Writing Wild: Forming a Creative Partnership with Nature*

**Fiction**

*Cowboys Never Cry*

*Crybaby Ranch*

*Fairy Tale Blues*

# Tuesdays in Jail

## WHAT I LEARNED TEACHING JOURNALING TO INMATES

TINA WELLING

New World Library
Novato, California

New World Library
14 Pamaron Way
Novato, California 94949



Names and details of characters have been changed to protect privacy. Some characters are composites.

Text design by Tona Pearce Myers

Library of Congress Cataloging-in-Publication Data

Names: Welling, Tina, author.
Title: Tuesdays in jail : what I learned teaching journaling to inmates / Tina Welling.
Description: Novato, California : New World Library, [2022] | Summary: "A novelist and writing teacher reveals the inspiring life lessons that she gained from over ten years of teaching weekly journaling classes to inmates at her local county jail. Themes include self-esteem, anger, compassion, and the power of forgiveness"-- Provided by publisher.
Identifiers: LCCN 2022021761 (print) | LCCN 2022021762 (ebook) | ISBN 9781608688319 (paperback) | ISBN 9781608688326 (epub)
Subjects: LCSH: Welling, Tina. | Authors, American--21st century--Biography. | Diaries--Authorship--Therapeutic uses. | Writers' workshops--Wyoming--Jackson Hole. | LCGFT: Autobiographies.
Classification: LCC PS3623.E4677 Z46 2022 (print) | LCC PS3623.E4677 Z46 2022 (ebook) | DDC 813/.6--dc23/eng/20220520
LC record available at https://lccn.loc.gov/2022021761
LC ebook record available at https://lccn.loc.gov/2022021762

First printing, September 2022
ISBN 978-1-60868-831-9
Ebook ISBN 978-1-60868-832-6
Printed in Canada on 100% postconsumer-waste recycled paper

New World Library is proud to be a Gold Certified Environmentally Responsible Publisher. Publisher certification awarded by Green Press Initiative.

10 9 8 7 6 5 4 3 2 1

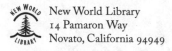

*Out beyond ideas of wrongdoing and rightdoing,*
*there is a field.*
*I'll meet you there.*

*When the soul lies down in that grass,*
*the world is too full to talk about.*

*Ideas,*
*language,*
*even the phrase "each other"*
*doesn't make any sense.*

Rumi, "A Great Wagon"

# [ Contents ]

Introduction.......................................................................xi

Tuesdays in Jail...................................................................1

Epilogue...........................................................................157

Workbook.........................................................................161

Acknowledgments.............................................................181

About the Author...............................................................183

# [ Introduction ]

One summer seven years ago, I began to conduct journaling workshops at the jail in Jackson Hole, Wyoming, where I live. It became a process that rippled in waves from a source hidden in the deep unseen and beached in surprising places. People asked me, "What made you think to begin journaling workshops in the Teton County Jail?" I never knew the answer, though I usually served one up from pieces and parts I mashed together and breaded into a whole, like a fish stick. I would point to my interest in Joseph Campbell, the scholar of myth who alerted us to the hero's journey, and tell how I was convinced that incarceration was a vital part of that life pattern — or, at least, it could be if used well. Or I would say that being an author began with journaling and that I believed it to be a direct pathway to self-awareness. Or I would report that nobody else from the community was doing anything for the inmates, so the bar seemed low enough for me to try something.

All the above was true. Yet years after beginning the workshops, I realized I had somehow stumbled onto a path that filled my days with meaning. Purpose, something I hadn't known I wanted to find, clarified choices about how to live, use my energy, spend my time. A sense of purpose can shine a piercing light on our values. In time what that light exposed shifted many things for me.

Surprises emerged over the next seven years. The biggest one was that the inmates and I had a lot of characteristics in common. It's just that they had been arrested and I had not. In our workshop we discussed self-esteem, anger, forgiveness, compassion for ourselves and each other, personal power, co-dependency, and so much more. It's true: we teach what we need to know.

Another surprise arose.

The inmates elevated the expectations I had in my relationships with everyone else. The intensity of our exchanges on Tuesday nights set a standard that seeped into my encounters with friends and family. Maybe that wasn't fair. The workshops were almost impromptu sessions of intimacy and vulnerability that none of us — neither the inmates nor I — could prepare for. The inmates didn't know what to expect from me when led out of their cells by armed officers, and I didn't know who I'd see or even how many inmates would be attending the workshop until we were face-to-face. That setup meant we were all taken unaware, and so we dropped into an immediate and raw authenticity. And why that happened instead of us all attending with our shields in place, I can't explain. For me, I was sitting in a circle with incarcerated men and feeling completely inadequate, so I went with whatever occurred in my thoughts and emotions and came out my mouth, an indication of how seat of the pants I was operating. For the men, this one hour a week was their only shot at exploring their inner lives within some framework and with others struggling alongside them.

With strict time allotted, we had no interest in falseness or manipulation or excuses. We headed straight for the core, and every one of us was exhausted at the end of our time together. Exhausted, but with a glimpse of peace.

So to lay such expectations on my friends and family may not have been appropriate, but I found myself leaning toward people who were more capable of going where the inmates and I traveled each week.

More surprises surfaced. Most came in smaller doses. Some took me years to absorb or even to notice. Others slammed me over the head and kept me from sleeping nights. All the surprises stretched me to the point of aching emotional muscles and loosened my heart into new agility. I could absorb more of life now, the sufferings and the satisfactions, and I was grateful for that.

Many of the wisdom teachings I've studied included the idea of becoming comfortable with not-knowing. Not my way. I liked to plan, and I liked to experience results for my efforts. Stories needed endings, relationships needed evolving, actions needed results. In the case of the jail workshops, not-knowing was the rule. I never knew what happened to the men after they left the Teton County Detention Center. No happy or sad endings to the stories I listened to, no endings at all. One day I would enter the tower or the grated lockdown room where we met for our workshops, and a regular would be missing. He had been released or sent to a rehabilitation center or moved to a prison. Every inmate related to me their intentions, hopes, dreams, and fears. But I never learned how they played out.

In conducting the workshops, the path opened up step-by-step. Yet, like tracking a moose in snowfall, if I didn't keep going, the hoof prints would fill in and leave me without direction.

# Tuesdays in Jail

# [ Chapter One ]

Eight p.m., and still light outside. The air felt warm and daisy-petal-soft on my arms. Like Navajo stonework, a band of turquoise was inlaid into the darker lapis lazuli of the sky and outlined the nearby mountains. Inside the entrance of the Teton County Detention Center, I lifted the phone and identified myself.

"Here for the journaling workshop."

An officer answered. "I'll buzz you through." I heard him announce to someone, "She's here."

I performed a clumsy gymnastic maneuver: hung up the phone with my left hand, slung my heavy canvas bag to that hand and leaped toward the locked door several feet away in time to reach the handle with my right hand during the brief buzz that signaled it was unlocked. If I didn't work it just right, I was spread-eagled with one foot in the open door and the phone not cradled properly. Seven years of Tuesday nights, and I was still working on my timing.

Inside the waiting room, I set down my bag. It held my notebook, ten journals, and a handful of pencils — short yellow pencils, designed for keeping golf scores. The rules. Also no spirals, no hardbacks, no staples, no paper clips, no computer or cell phone.

After I shrugged out of my jacket, a brown-uniformed sheriff's deputy came to lead me through five more locked or coded doors. This was the ritual in order for me to meet with a group of inmates for our workshop. I came fortified with a two-inch-thick file of journaling exercises and quotes that encouraged interest in looking inward. I told the inmates — most always men, only occasionally women — that this was where freedom was found. Which, of course, was true no matter which side of the locked doors we were on.

Each of the five doors needed keys or a code in order to pass through; each was made of thick metal and slammed closed with a deep clang that echoed off the cement-block walls. My stomach tightened with increasing discomfort as each door shut with finality behind me. I couldn't find my way out of this place even if I held the ring of keys and the memory of codes.

I followed behind the officer, who was wearing a bulletproof vest and a holster, through hallways, an elevator, and sometimes a dark spiral staircase wedged into a narrow shaft. I stepped into a place called the tower. The last door clanged and locked behind me.

And I was in the belly of the whale.

Joseph Campbell said about this phase of the hero's journey: "The belly is the dark place where digestion takes place and new energy is created." Journaling provided a tool for this process. Campbell also said this mythic theme of the hero going into the dark often resulted in his coming out transformed. The chance to witness such an event brought me back week after week. The same also applied to me: I went into the jail workshops and came out changed, every time.

The tower was a two-story room with no windows. A balcony ran along one side, and often a guard would walk there overlooking our circle as I conducted the workshop. On the other side, halfway up the wall, a window with black glass bowed out into the space, and behind that another officer operated all the controls — locks, lights — and watched everything through monitors. It felt like a fortress here. I didn't like institutional places, I recalled at this point each week, as if it were a brand-new thought. I liked creeks and trees. I lived in a log cabin.

The officer looked up toward the window, spoke into his lapel mic, and said, "Send them out." The wide heavy doors opened from cell blocks B and C. Several men in striped pants and shirts stepped out.

Abruptly all unease within me vanished and I was where I enjoyed being each Tuesday night.

I stepped forward to greet the inmates I knew, happy to see their familiar faces. To those men I hadn't met yet, I extended my hand and introduced myself. In jail only last names were used, so I asked for the men's first names and then said them often. We pulled gray plastic lawn chairs into a circle, and I passed out notebooks and pencils. The armed deputy leaned against a pillar behind me. The concern, a sergeant told me once, was that I could be taken hostage. But I never felt threatened.

Everyone received two short yellow pencils. Less than four inches long, no eraser, and they needed sharpening every few sentences. I bought the journals in a variety of colors and made a big deal out of having them choose one — inmates weren't offered many choices.

I asked one of the new guys, "James, what color for you?"

"I don't care. Any color."

"Hey, this may be the most excitement that comes your way all week," I joked. "Don't pass it up." I asked him, "What's your favorite color?"

"Blue, I guess."

I handed him a royal-blue speckled notebook.

"Raymond?"

"Yellow, please. It'll match my pencil."

We all laughed, and I was happy we were starting off so well.

I set the seventy-nine-cent plastic pencil sharpener on the floor in the middle of our circle. I'd been warned to make sure I never left it behind. It was true that a year earlier one man had held it up close to his face and studied it for a long time, finally sticking a fingernail into the screw, testing its looseness. That was when I realized the blade could be removed, so once I got home that night I dropped a dot of super glue on the screw head.

Sometimes I wondered what I was doing here, talking to inmates about their past lives, present incarcerations, and future hopes. What did I know?

The answer, it seemed, was just barely enough for the hour or two that I spent with the inmates each week. In this jail, inmates stayed no more than a year. If sentenced longer they were sent to a state prison. Most inmates stayed a few months. Any longer, and my guidance would be sorely tested. I had no training, no degrees that would be helpful, no experience in the areas of crime or addiction. The best thing I had going for me was that I was a decent cheerleader… and that the inmates had no one better showing up. That was how I got myself past the challenge that my mental judges set up for me periodically when they asked with sarcasm: "Who made you queen of the tower?"

Once notebooks and pencils were passed out, the workshop began.

"What are your good qualities? Make a list. Be generous with yourself. It's important to become conscious of our positive characteristics."

I waited until the little yellow pencils stopped moving around the circle before I went on to the next journaling question. They were all about self-esteem tonight. Afterward I asked the men what they had answered for the first question.

Mike, who had been incarcerated for five and a half months now, raised his hand to read his list first.

"Interested in other people. Like to be helpful. Good at math." He looked up. "Really good at math." He continued. "Stick with a job until finished and done right. Smarter than my foster mothers always said I was." He laughed. We'd heard about the number of foster homes Mike was sent to as a kid. Now at twenty-nine, he was beginning to separate himself from the reputation that followed him from one home to the next: "Brains useless as a bag of dog shit" was one way a foster parent had put it.

Mike said, "I'm thinking better about myself lately. I used to figure I could only get the two o'clock girls, you know?" The guys laughed, but I was lost. Mike said, "You know, at the bar. Closing time. Maybe I could get the only girl left to come home with me. These guys know what I mean."

Lots of agreement around the circle. I pictured the scene, last call, and Mike checking off girl after girl as each one left with someone else.

He said, "But I don't think I'll feel like that anymore. I know I'm still fucked up — oh, sorry — but I've got good things to offer a nice girl. I'm a good listener. Got some manners. I'm not all fucking bad — oh, sorry."

I didn't tell these guys that the first full sentence my son said when catching our cat on the kitchen counter, was: "Got the little blastard." The men liked to exercise their best selves with me. I appreciated that.

"Miguel, how about you? Read the list of your good qualities. When we say them out loud, we're really claiming them."

"I couldn't think of any."

I was startled but covered up. "None?"

"No." He shrugged. Miguel was new to the group. Only nineteen. Arrested for possession, possibly selling. His hair was shiny black; his skin was flawless. He seemed shy and kept his head down.

"Well, I just met you, but already I've noticed some good qualities about you."

Miguel looked up at last.

I said, "You treat the other guys well. They seem to like you." The group murmured in agreement. I held up two fingers. "That's two: you're nice and you're likable."

Miguel dipped his head again, but I saw he was smiling.

"While the group talks for the next few minutes, write down the names of three people you admire, and make a list of the qualities you like in them."

James was also new, arrested just last week. He was a handsome, strong-looking guy in his early forties. The newspaper reported he was driving under the influence, with an open container in his vehicle and a loaded pistol on his lap. He was in a national park, and at the time that was a federal offence. He began to speak and choked up.

"I've served five missions in Afghanistan, been shot three times, everything hurts, and all I need is a break from that once in a while. So I get in my truck, drive where it's beautiful, park someplace, and tip that bottle until I feel better." I didn't ask about the pistol. "I've been using drugs and alcohol for most of twenty years. My kids have grown up, left home, and I missed their entire lives — gone on a mission or drugged up. This is the first I've been completely sober all this time. I don't have nothin' on my list. But I'm going to. I'm going to start living like I got something for a list." And then he quietly let the tears stream.

We were hushed. I looked around the circle, and like me, the others were too choked up to say anything. After a moment, a couple of the men said, "Thanks, man." The rest nodded. Mike patted him on the back.

I wanted to honor him in some way. I said, "James, you are a warrior. You've fought for our country, and now you'll take that warrior energy and direct it to yourself."

James glanced up, nodded at me, and tipped his face to each shoulder of his shirt and wiped his tears.

"Miguel, back to you. What've you got?"

"My grandfather; he's dead now. My little brother; he's six. My one aunt."

"Good. Tell us their qualities."

He kept his head down but listed: he learned how to fix a lot of stuff from his grandfather and about happiness from his little brother, and his aunt let him live with her when he was kicked out of his family's house by his mother's new husband.

"Here's the big news, Miguel. You own all those qualities or the potential for them, or you wouldn't be recognizing them in others. So you can add to your list that you know how to fix things, you hold the ability for happiness, and you are a welcoming person, friendly, like your aunt."

We were all drained. I glanced over my shoulder at the officer behind me, and he nodded that time was up. He approached, ready to escort me out of the tower. The men and I stacked the gray plastic chairs and stored them against the wall. I passed out extra pencils to any who needed them. The men were led back to their cells, and I was taken to the first of the six locked doors.

In the elevator, after a bit of silence, the officer said, "They're all good guys."

I agreed.

# [ Chapter Two ]

I read about Liam in a newspaper report. He had been arrested over the weekend for being an inebriated pedestrian and was sent to court. There he yelled profanities at the judge, including the f-word. He was warned but continued, ever louder, ever more profane. With each outburst the twenty-four-year-old was sentenced an additional two weeks over his originally brief overnight detention.

I was appalled. I couldn't imagine anyone yelling the f-word in a courtroom directly at a judge, much less doing it repeatedly. Liam's behavior put him in maximum security, according to the newspapers. I knew that meant a twenty-four-hour solitary lockdown, with one hour each day to shower, use exercise machines, and grab a couple of books. I met with maximum-security inmates individually in a locked-down situation.

I sent a tiny prayer: Please do not let this man request to meet with me Tuesday night. I figured if he exhibited this level of disrespect and lack of self-control with a judge, I wouldn't have a chance.

First thing Tuesday night, the officer greeted me in the lobby of the detention center and said, "We got this guy in max ready for you in CV 2." And he gave me his last name.

I said to myself, "Oh, crap," and hoped my lips weren't moving.

The officer spoke into his lapel mic, "Charlie Victor 2." And the door unlocked with a loud buzz. I went in and there he was, sitting in a plastic chair on the other side of the metal grate in the small locked-down room. He was good-looking, young, dark-haired. He wore the pants and shirt assigned to maximum-security inmates — mustard-yellow — bright and gaudy as a caution light. The heavy door in my side of the room clanged shut behind me and locked. We exchanged names and without thinking about it, I began to tell him a story I'd heard. I didn't know if the story reflected reality, but the message was solidly true.

"There's a tribe in Africa that believes every person is born good. When someone does something hurtful and wrong in the community, they take the person to the center of the village, and the entire tribe comes and surrounds him. Each person tells the man every good thing they can remember about him from the time he was born. Because they believe he's just forgotten."

Liam dropped his head to his chest. I knew tears were falling. Tears welled in my eyes too.

After a bit of silence, he said, "It's good to know somebody understands."

Maybe the story about the tribe and the village was just one of those fictional reports popping up on the internet; it didn't matter. The story let Liam know there was compassion in the world. Somewhere.

I scooted my wooden chair, with the ratty orange upholstered seat, in closer to the grated window. I said, "Our culture doesn't hold that practice, so we have to remind ourselves about all our good qualities on our own."

I had given the officer a journal and two yellow golf pencils, and he unlocked the door on Liam's side and handed those to him now. I said to Liam, "This week, list all your good qualities in your journal. Fill pages." I assigned this to many inmates and never tired of seeing a man's face light up the following week when he reported his discoveries.

Often the men in maximum security chose to meet with me because it was the only chance they got each week to talk to someone. And I liked it because intimacy was easily reached during these one-on-one meetings. Since the maximum-security sentence extended to at least a month, we got the opportunity to build a good relationship. That happened with Liam and me. He was never disrespectful but always straightforward, soft-spoken. Soon he opened up about his life back home.

Liam had a sister. He said she was quite beautiful, two years older than him, and was diagnosed schizophrenic but refused to take her medication. The two of them lived with their mother, who was rarely home. Liam felt responsible for his sister.

"She brings men back to the house who are homeless and dirty." He hung his head.

I choked up. Kept silent. Wished I could reach through the metal grate to put my hand over his.

"She walks them right past me to her bedroom. She won't stop. I'm so afraid for her. I feel...I don't know..." He hung his head.

"Powerless," I said.

Liam raised his eyes. "Yeah. These guys are scary, doped up. They're filthy. I just feel like I can't stand it sometimes." He dropped his head again, then looked up. "I beg her to take her medicine."

"What about your mother? Can she help?"

"She works, goes to the bar, comes home drunk. She's no help." Liam shook his head. "I'm no help either. I'm a failure."

Suddenly an image arose of Liam yelling at the judge. I thought to myself, this kid got himself arrested so he could take a break from this burden. In order to ensure he wasn't just given a fine, credited with time spent incarcerated over the weekend, and released, Liam consciously or, more likely, unconsciously set up a situation in which he could rest and pull himself together.

I said, "It's so damn sad and frightening how your sister has chosen to disregard herself. But Liam, you can't be responsible for her. That's why you feel you're failing her. Because she has guaranteed no one can possibly succeed in helping her."

He nodded, wiped tears.

"In your library upstairs, when you get your break tomorrow, look for the book *Codependent No More.* You will feel like it's talking directly to you. You are not alone in feeling the way you do. Your predicament is unique and especially horrible, but there is a way to deal with it. Get the book."

I made a mental note to read Melody Beattie's clarifying book again myself. It was something I did periodically. And every time it was a fresh reminder of how I was, by default, codependent. Even sitting in CV 2 I was struggling not to solve Liam's life for him. Suggest he move away from home. Find something he loves doing, do it a lot, give his attention to himself. On and on. Better get that book out tonight.

After a few weeks in solitary confinement — an inhuman, often devastating experience that itself encouraged mental illness and was typically used only for the violent inmates — Liam regained strength and found a new balance. He was managing the isolation well. He read a lot and wrote in his journal. No one came to visit him. He was a stranger in town; his friends and family lived five hundred miles away.

"I feel like crap about how I treated the judge," Liam said one night. "I was way out of line. I yelled at that man." Liam said he was due to go to court again that coming Thursday and he felt embarrassed at how disrespectful he had been toward the judge. "I might not be allowed to say anything in court, so I don't know how I can make it up to the guy."

I didn't know if this was a good idea, but I suggested that Liam write a letter to the judge saying just how he felt and apologizing. I added, "I don't even know if that's something that's legally allowed."

Liam wrote the letter. Went to court on Thursday. And the next Tuesday he was no longer in jail. I asked an officer what had happened.

"Blew us all away. They uncuffed his hands in court without any explanation and said he was free to go. I don't know what the heck happened. But nobody goes from max to freedom. Not since I've been on the force."

When I met with the workshop group I asked if anyone had been in court on Thursday. I heard the same version: "A cop came to the cell where we were all waiting in handcuffs to see the judge; he uncuffed that guy, and the kid walked!"

I've thought of Liam often over the years. I hoped that his life was fulfilling, that his sister was taking her meds, and that his mother was sober, but I knew the unlikeliness of all that. Still, I was convinced that whatever was going on in his household, Liam was managing it better than before his incarceration. He had made sure of that before leaving there.

# [ Chapter Three ]

After living in Ohio all our lives, my former husband, our two young sons, and I moved to Cheyenne, Wyoming. While loading up the furniture, I discovered our younger son had used the back of his dresser as a journal. During the occasions when I'd sent him to his room for a time-out, he'd written in crayon that I was "not a fair mother," that he was "mad at me," that really it was his brother's fault, and maybe he'd run away. I liked finding this journal of my son's thoughts and emotions; it proved to me the value of giving him time-outs: he learned to go inward, listen to how he felt, and to express it. Paper and pencil would have been more appropriate, but parents can't ask for everything.

This may have been the seed of the journaling workshops I conduct in the jail. If so, it took the years of my two sons growing up and the years I needed to grow up myself for that seed to sprout. In fact, it took decades before one day, seemingly out of the blue, I outlined a plan and handed it to the sergeant at the detention center.

Studying the work of Joseph Campbell nourished the ground for that seed to sprout, leaf out, and flourish. Time-out was part of the hero's journey. Campbell referred to it most often as the belly of the whale, naming this experience after the biblical story of Jonah, because many cultures shared a similar parable. It denotes a time when a person doesn't recognize who they are in the situation they've found themselves in.

It has happened to all of us one way or another: we go along tending to our lives, and then abruptly we are pulled out of the familiar and land in a place of new demands. We become ill, we move to a strange community, enter a different career or job, find ourselves unprepared for parenthood or caretaking elders, and the list goes on. We put these periods to their highest use when we travel inward.

When men or women are arrested, individual identities are wiped out, personal belongings are taken away, and clothing is replaced with uniforms. No longer surrounded by friends or family, inmates are locked into a cell either alone or with strangers. Being jailed epitomized the belly of the whale segment of the hero's journey. To me, journaling about one's inner life was an experience far more valuable than merely waiting out the time, as many inmates considered doing. And it was far more important an experience than a legal punishment for crimes large or small, as society viewed it.

Fortunately the sergeant of the detention center felt the same way. I began volunteering to conduct weekly journaling workshops on Tuesday nights in August 2011, and my belief was proven correct: enormous inner work could be accomplished during this time-out. The way I saw it, the belly of the whale period may be the most important in a person's life: everything that happened before led up to it, pointing in the direction of needed development, and everything after was shaped by it.

Briefly, the hero's journey goes like this: a person hears a call and leaves their home to follow it into the world. There they meet friends and enemies, challenges and opportunities. Next comes a time of being pulled off the path, a time to gather self-knowledge and personal power, a time to become stronger. Because once released from this period, the person again meets friends and enemies, challenges and opportunities. But the idea is to do this on a higher level, from a place of strength arrived at through self-awareness.

Ultimately the goal of the hero's journey is to find what our myths call a boon, meaning a skill, a gift, wisdom, or perspective, something the hero brings back home. The boon may contribute to the community's enrichment, the way a student leaves home and returns as a teacher. Or the boon may be that the hero is personally lifted and in lifting himself lifts everyone around him.

That was how I saw Luis's experience of being incarcerated. Luis was a carpenter and family man in his early forties when he was arrested for dealing drugs. He came to the journaling workshop his first week in jail, despite knowing scant English. I led the group in some journaling exercises regarding self-knowledge, a particular challenge for inmates who had been addicted to drugs or alcohol for many years by the time they were arrested. As the men became sober, they began to remember themselves, their past dreams and intentions. This was the beginning of new hope coming in and thoughts about making changes in their future.

I said, "Number one: Write about one thing you feel especially proud of accomplishing during any time in your life."

Once the little yellow golf pencils stopped moving, I asked Travis to read his response first.

Travis said, "Raising my little girl all by myself. One day

when she was four, her mother dropped her off and then disappeared for the next few years. I didn't know how to brush a little girl's long tangly hair or anything."

I said, "What a challenge."

One of the other guys said, "I'd of found some scissors real fast."

We all laughed.

Except for Luis. He broke into sobs. He said, "I've been using cocaine all the years I am a man and in that time my kids they all grow up. I miss everything." He told us he had two sons, nineteen and eighteen, and two younger daughters, eleven and thirteen. "I spend all the years working two jobs and getting my drugs. All this time and now is only time I don't use the drugs. Sometimes I also drink too much. The whole time I be a man I am using drugs and I am drinking too much and I miss everything. This week only I am here fully and I see what I have done."

His face streamed with tears, and he didn't hide them or wipe them away. "I am nothing now."

"Luis, you are awake now," I said. "You are being honest now. You have begun a life of being everything you intended to be."

The other men agreed, "Yeah, man." A couple of men patted Luis on the shoulder.

During the next weeks of our journaling workshop, Luis became more and more honest with himself. His language skills increased so that he could talk comfortably with both English and Spanish speakers. Soon he was consoling others who felt shame and guilt over their choices and behavior and the fact that they were jailed. Many nights, driving home from the workshop, I felt uplifted by Luis's words and offered myself loving acceptance about my own poor decisions and actions.

But Luis's challenges weren't over. One day, after five months of incarceration, Luis's brother arrived for visiting hours and gave him some hard news. It had been a mystery why Luis's old friend, who had been arrested with him, had been released after a few days. Now he learned that this friend had given evidence against Luis, thereby erasing his own sentence and lengthening Luis's to many years in prison, followed by deportation. Luis had sold drugs to his friends, and this friend had turned informer.

This betrayal laid Luis low. Now a whole new battle raged within him. He suffered depression and anger and a deep sadness over this friend turned traitor. That such an old friend, one he'd known since childhood growing up in their Mexican village, would destroy Luis's life to this extent to get himself out of jail early was almost beyond Luis's ability to hold.

What Luis taught us about next was forgiveness.

In the journaling workshop we witnessed Luis struggle with his friend's betrayal and then with the realization that forgiveness was the only way out for him. I offered journaling prompts and brought in quotes that had helped me with my own struggles with forgiveness. One of my favorites was by author Jonathan Lockwood Huie: "Forgive others, not because they deserve forgiveness, but because you deserve peace."

Finally one day Luis said, "I have forgiven my old friend in my heart. But my mind remembers and feels sadness. Sometimes anger. But I can let it pass more easy now. I did wrong first. I took the drugs many years."

Just as Luis benefited from time alone working on his inner life, I too benefited from time spent in solitude. I'd learned from the inmates that it was imperative for my personal growth to respond to social invitations occasionally by answering, "I have another commitment." And that meant a commitment to myself.

Winter and summer, I loaded my backpack with my journal and lunch and skied or hiked to a place where I could make camp for the day and be alone. I have learned, along with the inmates, that meaningful time spent inward allows the process of bringing what lies in the dark of our unconscious, where it worked us, to the light of our consciousness, where we could work with it.

That was the gift of time-out in the belly of the whale.

# [ Chapter Four ]

The idea, taught by wisdom teachers around the world, that our inner lives are reflected in our outer lives, had mostly confused me. Besides, I found that was a difficult idea to hold at times and often way more responsibility than I was up for accepting.

I've known people who hold negative worldviews — everybody is out for themselves, people are greedy, you can't trust anyone — and had watched as they were proven correct. Their belief systems attracted the evidence of their perspectives.

After several years of seeing inmates weekly, I began to recognize I'd found a shortcut to my own inner development through learning that life mirrors us back to ourselves. The inmates invariably reflected back to me in exaggerated ways my own issues, my own stopping places, or as Jungians call it, my shadow.

Sometimes I wondered why I so eagerly grabbed my coat, zipped out the door, and drove to the jail on Tuesday nights when it meant that I was forced to confront my flaws. There they were, personified in the inmates who had been arrested for them.

The other night, Gerald and I met alone for thirty minutes.

He was a tough guy, big build, strong, tattoos running up the length of both arms, light scruffy beard, in his midthirties. Previously, as part of a group workshop, he came across as self-confident, responding to journaling exercises with unassailable answers that assured the group he was self-knowing, aware, content, happy. With just the two of us, I felt more comfortable challenging his remarks.

"So, Gerald, tell me one thing you really want," I said, once we had each settled in our locked-down sides of the grated room.

"I got everything I want," he said, then added, "except getting out of here."

I pushed him a bit, recalling all his past responses from his life-is-great attitude. "There must be something you want that you haven't yet gotten for yourself."

Gerald said, rather off-handedly, slouched down in his gray plastic chair with his legs crossed, looking vaguely disinterested, "I want my family to feel proud of me."

"Oh, heck," I said, "that's not in your reach."

Gerald scooted his butt back into the seat, straightened his back, and became alert, bobbing his head up to look at me directly. Getting his attention wasn't my point, but now that I had it, I went on to say that we needed to be true to ourselves and to let go of how others viewed us, since we had no control over that. Though, I confessed, when I loved someone, I wanted that person to understand me.

Gerald's blue eyes expressed depths of intelligence when he was interested in the conversation. He began to tell me how, despite all he had done to make his mother love him, she spoke to him cruelly, shunned him, and had poisoned his two older brothers against him, saying he wasn't a real part of the family. Gerald's chin wobbled. "She's mean to me."

Gerald was trying not to cry but was failing and, tipping his head side to side toward his shoulders, he wiped his tears on his red-and-white striped top. He said, "I feel abandoned."

It was heartbreaking to witness how a mother could inflict so much of her own pain onto her son. I said, "People make others feel the way they feel." And I touched on the idea of taking nothing personally, but Gerald was in too much pain to hear that. So I repeated his words. "You feel abandoned."

We were quiet for a few moments. Gerald wiped more tears away on his shirt sleeves. I pulled a tissue out of a small package I carried and pushed it through a slit used by lawyers to pass papers.

I asked him, "Would you say you abandon yourself in any way?" I was remembering the tool of reflection, how life mirrors us back to ourselves. Gerald assured me he didn't.

I asked, "Is addiction part of why you're incarcerated?"

He said, "I've used drugs off and on since I was a kid."

"Would you say using drugs was a way of abandoning yourself?"

Gerald was quiet a moment and then nodded in agreement and said drugs had messed up his life. The tears streamed down his face now, and he mopped them with the tissue.

He said, "Damn. Journaling class is rough."

He meant to be humorous and we both started to smile a bit, but there was too much truth in his words and we just held the silence.

When my throat unclogged, I said, "The thing about a parent being abusive is that we don't stop loving them, but we tend to stop loving ourselves." I added a few words about how we must supply ourselves with all we hoped to receive from others. Then an officer unlocked the door on Gerald's side of the grated room and cracked it open to signal that our time was over. Gerald and I stood up from our chairs. I held my hand, fingers spread, to the grate and Gerald matched my hand with his on the other side and we said our goodbyes.

Once I arrived home, it was late and I went to bed. Instead of counting sheep while lying there in the dark, I counted all the ways I had abandoned myself. Not maintaining my boundaries, overriding my emotions, saying yes when I meant no. I tossed the duvet off, pulled it back on, flipped from side to side, like, as my friend Libby says, "a hen on a spit."

And I thought to myself, Damn, journaling class is rough.

# [ Chapter Five ]

One Tuesday night I chugged up the elevator of the county jail with Officer Lana to conduct my weekly journaling workshop with the inmates. As usual, she had brought along a book to read. Her tastes in reading material ran to mass paperback mysteries. I asked what she was reading tonight. She held the book, a hardback this time, against her chest with the title hidden.

Lana said, "Oh, just a novel."

Now I was really interested. "What's the title?"

She took a moment as if she had to recall that information and even glanced at the book, tipping it two inches from her breast a second to refresh her memory. She answered, "Um, oh, it's *Fifty Shades of Grey.*" She latched her eyes straight ahead onto the elevator doors.

She said the title as if nobody would have heard of this novel. Like it was so obscure, I wouldn't know that she was planning to read erotica while being on guard during the workshop.

I only nodded and said, "I haven't read that." I didn't want to make her feel uncomfortable or, I should say, more uncomfortable. But could she possibly have thought I didn't know what the book was about? A book that had caused considerable discussion, had brought worldwide fame to an unknown author, and earned millions in movie rights?

Though truly I didn't care what she did during the workshop. I had always been at ease with the guys during my years of volunteering, never felt threatened or really in need of a guard. They were men from minimum and medium security and usually arrested for drug- or alcohol-related issues. But it was the rule in the jail that an armed officer must be in attendance, along with the officer behind the black glass in the control room. One minute into our workshop, and I was oblivious of all but the faces before me. I had even offered to hold the workshop with the men without a guard. But that was met with wide-eyed offense, as if I didn't get what a detention center was all about, and accompanied by the statement that it would be highly unwise, even dangerous, and definitely illegal.

The elevator bounced to a stop, and the doors opened into the large main room of the tower. Officer Lana and I stepped out.

Four maximum-security inmates sat in the plastic lawn chairs, waiting for me. I recognized them by their hot-mustard-colored uniforms. My step halted with one foot midair as if a film had stopped. I placed that foot on the cement floor and spun around to face Lana.

She refused to look at me.

Maximum-security inmates were kept apart from all other inmates and especially from each other. They were locked in solitude because of safety concerns. Whatever crime had brought them to jail involved violence. Either that or they had acted with violence to the arresting officers. Or if not that, they had a history involving violence. After seven years of conducting weekly workshops in the jail, I had never encountered a maximum-security inmate in any other situation than one at a time, each of us in adjoining locked-down rooms separated by a metal grate.

Now before me, four maximum security inmates sat altogether. And the armed officer was slinking off to the corner with her copy of *Fifty Shades of Grey*.

I'd always had trouble standing up for myself. I didn't like to swim against the current; I'd rather flow along with it. I'd make a good inmate, in fact. Would probably be on the inmate worker team because I was so amenable to others. So I simply pulled up my own plastic chair.

I said hi and introduced myself. As in AA meetings, I should have added, "And I'm a pushover."

I asked for each of their names. I made a point to remember names, because I knew they were important to us, but I couldn't seem to concentrate and failed to note a single one. I glanced over at Officer Lana. She was gone. Her body was there in the chair, but I knew the rest of her was in bed with Mr. Grey.

The men in the group were quiet. Or perhaps just stunned into silence like me. I stirred myself and gave my sales pitch on the value of self-knowledge and journaling as a power tool. I passed out notebooks and the little yellow golf pencils. I had brought along a set of questions for tonight's workshop, and I read the first one.

"When is it hard for you to say no?"

At first I didn't hear the irony of what I'd just said. With my eyes darting to the corner and back to the inmates, my body tense with a kind of readiness to lurch into necessary action at any moment, I had flipped into auto-drive and just read the page before me. But then I caught the meaning of my words. Never mind the inmates, could there be any more appropriate question for me right now? And the answer to the question, when was it hard for me to say no, was apparently in any situation at all, life threatening or otherwise.

Once more, I checked on Officer Lana. Despite the binding of her bulletproof vest and the black leather holster around her waist, she was now curled into the plastic chair she had dragged to the shadowy corner of the tower, a leg up and over one arm of it, her back slanted away from our group.

I realized another irony: the plot of her novel also involved that question. The heroine, I believed, had trouble saying no. Again, I hadn't read the book. I knew those of us who hadn't read it — and some of us who had — like to make clear to others that we knew very little about this novel. But people talked, and so most of us were aware this book was about bondage and dominance. Which led me to another irony: a female officer was reading a book about these subjects in a jail full of male inmates. But I couldn't go there; it was too unsettling.

While the men continued to write with their little yellow pencils in the journals I had given them, I cast my eyes up toward the control room that bowed out into the tower. I wondered about the guard behind the black glass who monitored rows of screens and the locks throughout the jail and who overlooked this space occupied by the four inmates and me. Usually that was Officer Kate. I hoped she was alert and paying extra attention. But what if she too was reading *Fifty Shades of Grey*? Curled into her own lawn chair, hugging the book to her chest, eyes inches from the page and not on the monitors or the tower room floor? I pictured Officer Kate moistening her lips, oblivious to her workspace duties in the same way Officer Lana was.

Still, even with one and possibly both armed officers likely in a state of mental and emotional absence from the detention center and instead residing in a lust-filled bedroom with

Mr. Grey, I no longer felt unsafe with these guys. We were doing well together in our pod of a journaling workshop. But I didn't feel at ease either. I was in a kind of uncertain limbo. Perhaps not unlike the limbo Officer Lana — and possibly Officer Kate — was experiencing, in that there was tension and the unknown ending. Yet there were also big differences in our limbos, and if given the choice, I would choose their tension and their unknown ending. Though, according to what I had heard about the book, the ending was never really unknown to the reader, to the heroine, or to Mr. Grey.

It was clear to me now that I needed to address my difficulty with saying no. When this was over, I would have to say no to the sergeant in charge of the night shift. I had long held a theory that the lessons we need to learn come around repeatedly until we face them and that each time they come around, they are more challenging. In fact, this was a topic the inmates and I often journaled about and discussed. Since I had passed up many chances to say no to family and friends, my challenge now was to say no to a police sergeant. Because although I believed I would make it out of the tower safely, I was not going to have this situation repeated. And for that to happen, I needed to stand up for myself and say a clear and definite no.

So while I wrestled with how I might go about saying no to the sergeant, I felt Officer Lana — and possibly Officer Kate — imagined how they might, if in the heroine's situation, go about saying yes to Mr. Grey.

As a footnote, the following Tuesday night I sought out the sergeant and, without my usual *ums* and *ahs*, said no to meeting with maximum-security inmates in a group ever again. He agreed quickly. I suspected by his briefly widened eyes that he had been unaware of the past week's event.

# [ Chapter Six ]

For the inmates, the journaling workshop stands out from their usual routine of predawn rising, abrupt room searches, empty hours between tasteless meals, and nightly bed checks. It offers relief from the shame and guilt and aimless caught-in-the-web sense of self so many inmates experience. It's a time when they can find and express their authentic selves. For much of the day inmates are switching between trying to stand their ground with the other inmates and acting submissively with the officers in charge. During this one hour every week, I invite them to tell me what they really think, feel, hope for, and fear. And I urge them to keep in touch with that authentic self by writing in their journals.

For me this hour pulls me out of my usual way of thinking about my life and sets me into thinking instead about life itself. The real beneath the routine. Each week my awareness widens, my heart opens, my intuition awakens. I try to be that ocean that Dogen, thirteenth-century Buddhist philosopher, wrote about, suggesting we can allow all to enter us and all to flow through us. It's a rare opportunity to experience as vast a vulnerability as I can crack myself open to hold. To be willing to meet whatever occurs with whomever comes into my circle of energy.

Since very little preparation is possible, this is the only way I know how to be there. Not knowing who will attend the workshop, what miseries or insights or stories are moving through the individual men, I can't do much to ready myself. I can only be as open as possible. I read the latest research and memoirs about addiction. I read spiritual books to stretch and strengthen myself. And then I put it all in a big salad bowl and douse it with lemon juice and honey, see how that tastes when faced with the actual beings struggling with it all.

My goal with the inmates is to remind them of that spirit spark — as an early beloved spiritual teacher of mine called it — that lies within them. Twelfth-century poet Hafiz said it well: "I wish that I could show you when you are lonely or in darkness the astonishing light of your own being."

I start there. I listen. I respond with whatever occurs to me to let the men know I see their astonishing light. I speak to that. Ask journaling questions intended to guide us all there.

Though we are separated either by a metal grate or, in the tower, by a circling armed guard, I think everyone gets that we're all in this thing called life together. That we're all imprisoned by something, and that most often it's our own narrow vision. I discuss that too with the inmates, those qualities within us that limit our awareness: anger, resentment, harsh self-talk, low self-esteem, addiction, sense of failure. I enjoy the company of these fellow explorers who are always eager to discuss what they have never or rarely put into language before.

Often the inmates have trouble with the concept of spirituality due to abusive or abandoning parents. They desire a connection with a guiding and loving force and yet flounder around in a field of resentment and longing. No wonder. When we are vulnerable toddlers looking up several feet into the face of our caretakers for food, emotional sustenance, shelter, and safety, we are looking into the faces of our gods. We adore them and want to become them and go to them to fulfill every need. If they ignore us, we feel unworthy of being seen. If they swipe an angry hand at us, we feel shame at not measuring up. In this unstable union we are without ground, have no certain point in which to find our bearings or from which to push off for our personal growth.

Our parents or caretakers, as our first gods, are our introductions to forces greater than ourselves. This is how we learn spirituality, how to have a relationship with the god of our world, whatever name it goes by: the Force, the Universe, Allah, the Greater Intelligence.

Jail can be a place for finding one's spiritual center. It's the solitude, the hitting bottom, the claiming of the past, and the fear and hope about what's next. Yet so many inmates have trouble here. They've rejected whatever religion or spiritual teachings loomed in their background, yet they still long for evidence of some greater being that will help usher in the best of them.

In our workshops I talk about the spiritual part of life without ever using the word *God* or other religious terms. I think about Zeke, who was clearly yearning and just as clearly turned off by anything that hinted of the unseen. He believed he was alone and that he alone would have to deal with whatever came his way.

I said, "Zeke, you're wearing cotton pants, but I see you wearing a cloud. And when I look further, I see rubber trees in South America."

Zeke joked, "Nope. Just pants. But I'll have some of whatever you've smoked."

We all laughed.

I said, "Take a thread from your pant cuff, and you can trace it all around the world. Recognize the fruits and vegetables grown in every part of the planet to feed the workers while they were farming and harvesting the cotton. The cotton plants were loaded onto trucks, the engines made of metals mined in Africa, and driven on tires made from rubber trees in the Amazon, taken to factories where it was created into cloth, then shipped again to outlets and finally here. Think how you are connected to the sun and the rain clouds needed for the cotton to grow in the fields and for the foods to grow in gardens to feed the workers. You are not alone here; you can trace your connection to every other thing on the planet by a single thread."

Jim said, "I want to believe in God. I really want that. And when my Aunt Nancy comes to visit and prays with me, I feel it. I'm enlarged by it. But then being here where nothing is beautiful or inspiring, I lose it. It's like these cement walls sponge it up."

We talk about the word *God* and how it holds so much negative energy for some. I suggest we exchange the word for *Life*, capital *L*. In many ways, we can't *not* talk about God or Life or sacred energy; we are It, and It is all around us, of us, in us.

That's what Ken was speaking about when he and I met alone one night in the grated locked-down room. He said, "There's a little black spider in my cell. When I scrub my floor, I'm careful not to disturb it. Sometimes it lives under the sink. Before coming to the workshop I watched it go down the floor drain. It does that sometimes. I don't know what it's got going down there. I left it two crumbs. One of hamburger and, in case it's a vegetarian, one of cornbread." He laughed at himself but clearly recognized he was engaged in a sacred exchange with Life.

In so many ways throughout our days, we are connecting to that astonishing light within us that Hafiz spoke of. Yet in just as many ways we spend our days unconscious of it. Bringing awareness of the sacred, the connectedness, the mysterious into our consciousness enhances our sense of aliveness. And, bottom line, that is what we all *really* want: a fuller sense of aliveness.

And so the inmates and I meet on Tuesday nights to remind each other to clear the way and to reach for that.

# [ Chapter Seven ]

One of the most potent journaling questions I used to ask the inmates was, When did you know you were strong enough to withstand pain, betrayal, disappointment, and whatever else life might present to you?

A. said, "When I came to Los Angeles, the largest city I had ever seen, from Mexico, at age eighteen, scared, alone, a stranger, not knowing the language. I had to find a job to pay for a room and food and send money home. It was hard," he said, "but then I knew what I could do."

S. said, "The time my dad tried to kill himself and I stopped him."

M. said, "When my brother raped me."

L. said, "When I watched my friend get shot."

K. said, "When I pleaded guilty to pedophilia, and it was really my dad who did it."

T. said, "When I came home from Iraq and got treated like shit by my country."

P. said, "When I made it to America from Mexico through the desert with my little brother."

J. said, "When my mom visited me in jail up in Sheridan

and accused me of ruining the family because of my drug use. And she was high."

B. said, "The last time my stepdad beat me."

N. said, "When my foster mom said I was nothing but a stinking pile of garbage and that I would be all my life."

H. said, "When I got shot in Afghanistan the first time."

D. said, "When I was sixteen and got kicked out of my home."

C. said, "When I was a little boy and got raped and no one believed me."

W. said, "I can't even tell you. It'd make you cry."

# [ Chapter Eight ]

January in Jackson Hole is the month most likely to hold days of severe subzero temperatures, sometimes a string of them lasting three weeks. Skies are often gray. The sun doesn't climb over Snow King Mountain and lighten my yard until midmorning, and at four thirty in the afternoon I am turning on lamps.

This January I traveled to my sister Gayle's house on the east coast of Florida. I planned to set myself up for my version of the belly of the whale — empty time and a lack of usual obligations. Away from my house with its demands for upkeep, apart from my beloved friends, I left my calendar at home and a message on my email server that I was out of reach. I was calling this a voluntary stay in the dark to, as Joseph Campbell said, digest and create. My tools were paper and pen. My setting was the bank of the south fork of the St. Lucie River, where Gayle's old Florida bungalow overlooked the brackish tidal waters. Gayle and her husband Bob had boarded a plane that morning for California, leaving Max, their giant golden doodle, and me in the house alone. The river flowed calmly past the deck where I sat at an umbrella table. Max was stretched in the shade at my feet.

My thoughts, to my surprise, flowed roughly, as if wind-whipped. A year had passed since I divorced my husband after five decades of marriage. I had expected by now to have settled all those mind and heart disturbances. After all, the decision itself hadn't been a mental process of pros and cons that I needed to argue about with myself; it was a clean knowing that arose smoothly one evening while my former husband and I were out on a dinner-and-movie date. And yet here I was choking back tears and trying to swallow my sip of coffee through a detour route around the clog in my throat.

I wanted to push back my chair from the umbrella table and go... shopping, walking, anything. Just go. I raised my eyes to the small island in the center of the river where an ibis wading on the beach illuminated the dark density of palm trees and palmettos. I thought about the inmates at the county jail that I saw on Tuesday nights and how I tell them to face the hard stuff, look at it, claim it as their own. They have nowhere to go, no feathered or furred companions to soothe the discomfort of sitting with their difficult memories. And though a rift in my heart yawned, raw and sore, I stayed in my seat.

As much as I'd tried to smooth it over for everyone — sons, daughters-in-law, siblings, and friends — by assuring them all that nothing big had changed, it had. Something big had changed.

I hired a carpenter to help us divide our house, give us separate entrances, two cooking areas. I tell people that it was more than a friendly divorce, it was a loving divorce, and that we shared our two pups, newspapers, and melons. Today I realized I had offered a gauzy storyline in which details were used to hide the truth while seemingly telling it.

We did share pups, newspapers, and melons. And yet while

I was busily assuring everyone with calming answers to their many questions, I forgot to listen to myself, to my questions, until now. Why, I wondered.

Several years back, during another visit to my sister's house here on the Florida coast, Hurricane Wilma came screaming through early one morning while I was still in my pajamas. Wind buckled the outer walls, curving them inward, forcing the refrigerator into the walkway of the kitchen. Rain pushed through the seams of the windows and filled buckets and pots. The St. Lucie left its banks and flooded the land around us, trapping us and our cars. Once I peeked out through a crack in the boarded glass doors and saw a cement wall of river water lifted forty feet high. The racket was tremendous.

And then it was silent.

We were abruptly in the eye of the hurricane.

We stepped outside like sleepwalkers, disbelieving the calm, the blue sky. Then we took in the mass of floating debris in the pool, the broken palm fronds and tree limbs on the lawn. We had fifteen minutes to strengthen our shelter and ourselves. We worked silently and fast, picking up fallen coconuts and potted plants from the decks that could turn into missiles, wreaking further damage when the wind reversed itself on the other side of the eye. We double-checked the boarded windows and doors, secured the boat. Quickly we ate peanut butter and crackers to fuel us for the next bout, as the eye passed and the spin of wind and water pummeled us again.

What made me think of that day? I had visited here dozens of times since then, with no threat of a hurricane. Then I made the connection.

The eye of a hurricane was the belly of the whale.

It was a time to repair and fortify.

Because once on the other side, life may slam us again with ferocity, and we must be ready.

Though I came to Florida for a time-out, I had also armed myself with goals and distractions. But I too needed to repair and to fortify. So I told myself: Put away your plans to polish that short story, begin the long-planned novel, sketch, and watercolor. You have more important work to do. And if you choose not to do it, you no longer have a right to spend Tuesday nights with the inmates. You will have nothing to offer them.

The next morning found Max and me on the deck again beneath the striped sun umbrella. Journal, pen, and coffee for me. A chew toy and a bowl of cool water for Max. On the island, the ibis had been replaced by a gathering of unseen birds creating a ruckus in the palms. A tiny lizard baked on the railing beside me, his coral dewlap pulsing like a sunbeam. I didn't miss my former husband. Yet I still felt a strong energetic connection, still felt psychically partnered. By habit, I wondered about him and sometimes worried.

Was that how my friend Caroline had been feeling since the death of her husband, still energetically married? A few months before I came to Florida, a terrible accident had occurred in my valley. Late Friday night a man driving a truck had veered onto the sidewalk, killing my friend's husband and injuring her and her younger brother.

The newspapers reported that the man who was driving the truck was intoxicated, had open containers of beer and tequila with him. He was driving in the dark with his headlights off, on the wrong side of the road. This man had a history of twenty-seven driving and traffic entanglements with the law in another state, some involving DUIs. He was incarcerated in our county jail. Tuesday night, days after the accident, he requested to meet with me. As he was held in maximum security, we met alone in the locked-down rooms connected by the metal grate. His name was Brodie, forty years old, married and father to a stepdaughter.

Before meeting this man, I felt anger simmering beneath my sadness. It seemed to me that a deep and dense denial allowed this person to ignore messages from life and from the authorities twenty-seven times, and now my friend's husband, a good man, an admired man in our community, was dead.

I encountered denial often with the inmates, people who preferred to blame the town, the cops, their friends, or their family for what they called their "bad luck" at being jailed. But his was the most extreme case of denial I had ever come across. I was aware that I taught what I needed to learn. That we were, every one of us, traveling the hero's journey, consciously or not. Yet after meeting with Brodie I believed I had never met with or experienced denial of such impenetrable density.

I felt empathy for him because of how sad and burdened he seemed and encouraged him to be kind to himself, but I questioned whether he had come to terms with his situation. The police were calling the event a homicide, yet Brodie referred to it as "an accident in which a man died," as if it didn't have much to do with him. Something about the way he said that created a gap between us; I didn't get the sense that he was fully present with his reality.

I took a sip of coffee. Reached down to pet Max. Ripples on the water suggested a manatee may be surfacing. I rushed to the end of the dock and watched but saw nothing.

And then it hit me.

I could look back to early adulthood and spot from this distance issues that I had refused to acknowledge — not twenty-seven times but that number and more in years. For years I had been in denial. I, who felt strongly about being truthful to myself, who examined my actions each day before sleep each night. I was shocked to my bones. I had been in deep denial. A denial of impenetrable density.

I felt restless.

I returned to the upper deck. "Max, want to go for a walk?"

His tail didn't even wag. He rolled his eyes up to me, while keeping his muzzle resting between his front paws. At home I had to spell the word, or eight furry legs whipped into a frenzy at the door. Max, along with my two at home, Emmett and Zoe, had themselves spent time in the belly of the whale. Animal shelters were a kind of limbo behind bars. All three dogs were rescued from abusive homes. Max was still leery of people, and since I visited only occasionally, it took more trust than he could muster to leave his yard with me.

I saw now that I had carried a kind of forbearance with my challenges that masked an inability to deal with them. Because if I dealt with them, I would have to be responsible for them. I had not faced, or acknowledged, or claimed many things.

And I had some work to do.

But where to begin?

Growing up, I had struggled to maintain a sense of self in a household headed by a strong, controlling man. My businessman father joked that although he intended to become the Big Tycoon in town, he came only close enough to call himself the Big Typhoon.

Humor helped everything. And masked much.

At seventeen and a freshman in college, I fell for an older art student who wore a sky-blue windbreaker and drove an old sedan with a rope that wove through the steering wheel, wrapped around his hand, and regulated the broken accelerator pedal. I thought I had found the exact opposite of my father. After my sophomore year I married him and took up being a wife in just the way my mother had: I leaned on him for every little thing. Which meant in the end that I took little responsibility for my life.

That man too made me laugh. The sexy mental exchange of humor between us distracted me from all that I wasn't ready to deal with in our relationship or within myself.

Caroline too depended heavily on her husband. Though I was allowed decades to grow into independence, she was abruptly yanked into it. She measured up majestically. While she was still suffering from her injuries and grieving the loss of her life partner, she testified on Brodie's behalf. She publicly forgave him, hugged him in court before the judge and both her and Brodie's families. By that time, she had learned, as I had, that Brodie was a gentle and burdened man and that once he was forced into sobriety through incarceration, he began to take full responsibility for his actions.

While sitting in the shade of the umbrella table I wrote in my journal that I had been given the gift of role models for facing my own harsh realities, and like Brodie, now sitting in a jail cell, I too could own responsibility for my actions or, more often in my case, inactions. And like Caroline I could offer forgiveness to others and to myself.

# [ Chapter Nine ]

Cameron was forty-three years old and said he'd been in jail off and on throughout his life. "But this is it. Not coming back," he told the journaling group. Seven of us sat in the lawn chairs that we'd scraped across the cement floor in the tower to form a circle. "I've been drug free for a year. Still, I messed up. I got some stuff for somebody. Trying to be a nice guy in the wrong way. Won't do that again."

Because every one of the men attending tonight struggled with addiction — drugs or alcohol — I introduced questions aimed at getting to who these men were before their addictions and their crimes. I made them laugh by describing what sweet, fat-cheeked toddlers they once were, years before life mangled their self-esteem and deflated their dreams.

I said, "You tried to walk and fell repeatedly on your diaper-padded butts, got up, and tried again. Seeing your image in a mirror made you reach out for that other baby. Your mother hiding behind her own hand made you hiccup with giggles. It didn't take much for you to find fun. Tell me in a few lines in your journals about your earliest memories playing."

I followed with four more questions about their early years, and then we talked about the responses they'd written in their journals. I called on Cameron first.

"Tell us about your earliest memory of playing."

He said, "I liked playing with Matchbox cars." The other guys nodded and smiled; they were remembering that too.

Cameron said, "Guess I was maybe three. And I'd make noises while pushing my Matchbox cars all around my mom and dad's bales of marijuana."

A few of the men gasped. A couple said, "Shit, man." I nodded for him to continue.

Cameron said, "That's been the family business since I was born."

I said, "You were breathing marijuana dust as a toddler."

He nodded. "All my life. Then smoked it, then graduated into the hard stuff."

"And now you've been clean for an entire year. That's impressive."

Cameron said, "And tough."

"I'll bet."

The others were respectfully quiet.

Then Allan said, "You didn't have a chance, buddy."

"I do now though. Got a good job in construction, staying clean, and not doing any more favors in that area. I should be out in a couple weeks, since all I did was point somebody in the right direction — I mean, wrong."

I wanted to give the others a chance to talk before our time was up. It was the most important part of our workshop — the chance to talk. This still amazed me at times, the desire, the need to talk about the intimate matters of the heart. That these guys would do so willingly, in front of one another — some strangers, some cellmates — was strong evidence that they had not been heard during their lives. Not heard by others, not heard by themselves. They had not often articulated their inner thoughts, feelings, memories, yearnings. Journaling allowed them to pin words to the elusive thoughts and emotions of their lives, and once named, they could be examined.

"Dell, what's your earliest memory?"

"Being moved from my grandma's house to some stranger's place. Foster deal. They kept trying to get me to sit up and play ball, but I just hid my head under my arms, lying on my stomach, knees under my belly. I was probably three or four."

"Bear protection posture," Billy said.

"Yeah." Dell didn't want to talk anymore. He was afraid he'd sob out loud, and we all knew it and carried on as if we didn't.

"Real fast around the circle now: Allan, question number four, what did you write for your childhood heroes and who you wanted to be when you grew up?"

"My uncle was my hero. He's in prison now, down in Arizona."

"Keith, what did you like to play when you were little?"

"We didn't have toys, but we played hard, my brothers and me. Played with dirt and rocks. We played bulldozer, that's what we called it."

"Albert?"

"Sports. Every kind. Baseball, basketball, football. Give me a ball, and I was a happy kid. Kinda miss it."

"Number five: What would you like to bring from your childhood into your adulthood, and how might you do that? Jerry?"

"That kind of safety you get to have figuring the adults must know what to do. I'd like to give that to my kids."

"Tony?"

"Yeah, me too. Instead they got a dad in jail."

"For now," I added. And reminded them this was their time to recall what they meant to do and be as men and partners and fathers and figure how to get there. "In many cases the adults never knew what to do," I said. "They were making it up as they went along. So maybe you could lower the bar for yourself. Make your intention attainable."

"You're right," Rafe said. "Half the time I was taking care of them. My folks were drinkers, always either hungover or drunk. That's how I remember being a kid. It didn't feel right when I was real little, but I just shut up those feelings and figured it must be right."

I walked out of the workshop and into the elevator with the guard, sadly impressed by how powerful the beginnings of our lives were. And yet I also believed that tonight we all came away with an awareness that we didn't need to keep carrying the old images of ourselves that didn't serve us well. They weren't essential parts of us but rather characteristics we might peel off.

The guard led the way through the locked and coded doors. I followed and got caught up in the memory of taking my father hiking during one of his visits to me in Jackson Hole. An activity he had never considered any time in his life living in either Ohio or Florida. My mother had died recently, and his life was unstructured — plenty of money and a dearth of interests. I would outfit him with a ball cap, backpack, lunch, and a water bottle, and we'd head to a mountain trail. One day we were coming down from Cascade Canyon, walking on a skinny steep path with rock and dust skittering beneath our feet and a forty foot drop-off inches away. My dad began to slip, and just before going over the edge, he fell on his butt.

"I'm fine. Go on." He gestured for me to move on down the path. "Go on," he demanded.

"Dad, no. Stop. Let's rest a second."

"Go on. Move now."

"Dad." I was shaken. We both needed to pause and pull it together.

Just then a woman who saw the near-disaster said, "I'm a doctor. Please, sir, just rest a bit before going on."

But my dad was embarrassed. Filled with self-consciousness and apparently feeling extremely uncool, unmanly, incapable, he would not rest for one second. He wanted to be upright and out of sight of anyone who had spotted the mishap.

Suddenly I saw the sometimes paralyzing self-consciousness I had carried from the time I was a young child, not as an actual part of me but as something learned, something taken on.

Then I realized: I could take it off.

Though I didn't need to take it off; it fell away of its own accord. Just dropped off me upon my awareness of it.

Too bad I was so taken with the abrupt clearing that I couldn't keep it to myself. I spent the rest of the hike down from Inspiration Point exclaiming over the realization out loud to the very man who did not want to engage in the subject of self-consciousness. But I was light bodied with the release of this decades-long encumbrance, this living outside myself and watching all my movements and expressions and judging each as lacking in grace.

Now out in the jail parking lot I saw it had snowed four inches while I'd been inside. I grabbed my ice scraper from the back floor of the car and cleared the windshield, side mirrors, and windows. As fast as I worked around the car, the snow covered up my cleared areas again. It felt good out there. Chilled air on my cheeks and expanding in my lungs. I breathed deeply, gave up the race with the snowfall, and got in the car. I'd creep my way home. The pace matched my thoughts.

I believed I'd witnessed Cameron seeing himself anew, possibly as not an addict by nature but by family tradition. Every once in a while that light came to the eyes of an inmate when he realized, in the same way I did about my painful self-consciousness, that he was not what his family told him he was as a child. Albert was not the selfish bastard his mother accused him of being; Dave was not the idiot that couldn't do anything right; Tony was not headed for a life in prison; Keith was not going to die an alcoholic like his father.

I don't think a person has to watch their father skid to the edge of a cliff to realize the false overlay of qualities plastered on during childhood. Personal inquiry often does the trick of helping us separate reality from our habitual perspectives. One such question the group worked with tonight was: When did you first realize you were different from your parents?

"When I learned I was going to become a dad. I knew I'd never act like my dad. I suddenly saw the role in a whole new way. How does a guy, a grown man, look at a baby boy and begin feeling in competition with him? How does that even happen?"

"When I made friends in school and went to their house to play. If they did something they shouldn't, they were sent to their room for twenty minutes, not beaten for that long."

"I never knew my dad, so I don't know how I'm different from him, except for one thing. I'll be around my kids every day, not take off before they're one."

Cameron seemed to have successfully peeled off the drug-supplier ID and his own addiction once he realized he didn't need to carry on the family business. Months after he left the jail, he and I spotted each other. Cameron was working at a construction site, which I happened to walk past one day. We caught each other's eyes and both stilled a moment and grinned widely. He looked healthy, happy, industrious.

• • • •

Inside the car I cranked up the heat and turned on the radio, set to NPR and playing classical music this time of night. I backed out of my parking spot and headed home.

And like almost every Tuesday night I wondered to myself — and tonight said out loud — "So what just happened?"

Because sitting behind the steering wheel, I felt myself descend back into myself. I am not implying an out-of-body experience but more of an out-of-my-normal-limits experience. It was as if the inmates and their need pulled out of me, or out of the shared ether, or out of the combined energy of us all, something I was not used to exhibiting in my everyday life. Neither do I mean to imply that something "woo-woo" had occurred. It was more the sense of being able to stretch to accommodate the situation. It was as if during an exercise class I discovered myself doing the splits when normally I was not limber enough even to touch my toes.

On Tuesday nights I was especially limber. Often during the two-mile drive home I couldn't recall what I had said to the inmates in the workshop. Though I could easily recall what the inmates had said to me, their stories and emotions.

We had only a short time in the workshop to deal with lifelong injuries and miseries, and so I blurted whatever occurred to me, tried to use the men's stories to direct them back to an enlarged, positive view of themselves. This exchanging of stories had to be more than a pity party. I wanted to empower the men who talked of their heart-hurt. By now I trusted that whatever I said was kind, carried intent to soothe and understand, felt true to me at the moment, and was buoyed by the desire to nudge them up one more notch into self-compassion and self-esteem.

But my experience in the car driving home was one of perplexity. A sense of accomplishment was mated with one of incompleteness — so much more to be said and understood — and all of it shrouded in a kind of mystery. Where did that burst of wise words gathered from some long-ago reading and long-ago forgotten come from? What I did remember from the exchanges with the inmates was my stance of stillness, of listening, of full-being acceptance, no matter the horror of the story details, and then scanning for the hidden kernel that held the life lesson. I felt fully aware driving home through the snowy night, but none of this awareness held language. I could not explain to myself what the hell had happened in the past couple of hours.

I didn't always sleep well on Tuesday nights. Sometimes a certain story stirred me into restlessness. Sometimes the various voices or emotions of the inmates wended through my thoughts as I tossed and pushed my pillows around. Invariably the discussion in my head turned personal, and I realized once again that I had been talking to myself and exploring my own issues, dredging up things about myself I had been unaware of until the inmates burrowed into my psyche. It was as though I was teaching myself what I didn't know I knew. Or was it that I actually didn't know it before saying it?

# [ Chapter Ten ]

I had sketched out a few questions for our Tuesday-night journaling workshop. Once I caught up on the men's news about their court dates, their visitors, and the books they were reading, we opened our journals and I briefly talked about personal power. I emphasized that it resided within, that no one could rob us of it. Despite a court system that seemed aimed at that goal, despite uniformed people with guns on their belts standing guard over them day and night. As the author and activist Alice Walker says, "The most common way people give up their power is by thinking they don't have any."

Tonight's question number one: Do you feel you are as good as everyone you encounter? "Jess, what did you put for that answer?"

"I put yes, before I came to jail, I felt like I was as good as my buddies and the guys I work construction with."

"But I want to know about now, today."

"Well, hell no. I'm in jail."

I said, "Jess, aim to get to the place where you feel good no matter where you are. You're in jail, so you made some decisions that didn't work for you, but that doesn't diminish you as a man who strives to live his life well. You're here. Be here.

And when you move on from here, you'll know some big things about yourself. And one of them will be that you can feel solid about your place in life, no matter where you are. That will do a lot toward giving you personal power. It's what we all want."

When I was talking to the men, I was aware that while they were in jail their noses were rubbed in the idea that they were powerless just about every minute. Along with the few guards who felt so bereft themselves of personal power that they needed to inflict their punishing attitudes on the inmates, the striped clothing, the orange slippers, the inability to hold back an apple from their lunch to eat later in the afternoon without punishment, all conspired to rob these men of their power.

Question number two: Write down the inner quality you feel is your strongest.

Nat said, "Patience."

Jess said, "Sense of humor."

Gary said, "Positive thinking."

Brodie said, "Gratitude."

"All good qualities that help considerably with holding a sense of personal power," I said. "And, as always, writing it down makes it conscious and available for use rather than an unformed idea floating around in the dark of the unconscious."

Next I asked a few more questions to build the idea that as inmates they held more control over their lives than the circumstances of being in jail suggested. The conversation that followed during our hour together revolved around feeling like either a survivor or a victim. The men all had faced severe difficulties in their lives, so I acknowledged that and asked each of them to write about how that served them or created their outlook.

Brodie, an admitted alcoholic, said he took full responsibility for his situation. Since our first meeting after his arrest for driving intoxicated and causing an accident that killed my friend's husband, Brodie and I have created a warm relationship. I'd discovered what a sincerely caring man he was. After many weeks of talking together I learned about the load of responsibilities he shouldered for his large extended family of elders and children, both in the states and in Honduras. I witnessed his deep remorse for his years of alcoholism and the damage it had done to others. He said now, "I am the one to cause this horrible pain and loss. Even my own family who loves me suffers from my behavior." For one thing, he could no longer help support them with income while incarcerated. But he said he felt like a survivor, someone who would pay for his bad choices and who could change his actions in the future. He was beginning to understand himself.

"I see the pattern of stress that built from all my responsibilities until I was in bad need of relief," Brodie said. "I'd start drinking beer and tequila. First only on the weekends, then I'd get worried about my relatives in Honduras and I'd get worried about the jobs I am in charge of getting done on time, and I'd worry about my workers doing things right, so I'd start to drink on Thursdays too."

Brodie was a gentle person; he spoke softly with a bare hint of an accent, and left to his own devices, he might have been an introvert. Yet his family, both here and in Honduras, needed financial help, and before his arrest Brodie was working as hard and as fast as he could to meet everyone's needs. That included his stepdaughter, who was headed to college, for which Brodie was building a savings account. His biggest dream was to own his own house to shelter the whole family.

Brodie continued. "From Thursdays I keep drinking on through the weekend. And then I was carrying the drinking on through Monday and finally all week long, and that's when I made the horrible mistake."

Brodie was awaiting his sentence and knew it could range from a couple of years to a couple of decades in the state prison. He was experiencing stress without the aid of alcohol right now. Even so, he had made the effort to write a letter to Caroline, expressing his sorrow and remorse over his actions that resulted in her husband's death and the pain she was still dealing with.

Gary said, "I am a survivor, because otherwise I'd be nothing at all. I can't stop fighting for a fair trial, or I'll be a victim sitting in prison for the next twenty years." He added, "But I've always been a survivor. Had to be, with my dad going off in alcoholic rages every weekend."

But what did being a survivor mean to Gary, Nat, Brodie, and Jess?

"It means that I'm not quitting," Gary said. "I'm going to be me." I asked Gary what he meant by that. "Keep going no matter what, that's the real me. I want to feel like a victim sometimes. I just want to go there to that victim place and sulk about how the prosecutor has it in for me and how the judge doesn't get who I am but just sees what he's already decided I've done before hearing me out. I just want to soak in the mean treatment I get sometimes. This shitty food, those guards looking at me like they think I got it too good. The way some of them look around my cell, trying to find contraband and how they turn up the heat real high when we complain about how cold it is. I can get stuck there. It's endless, that list of complaints. But then I think I might just die inside. And I have to pull myself up with some hope or some memories of how I once lived with good friends and good work and sailing on the weekends, you know?"

Nat was still a kid, twenty-two years old, and yet he'd been arrested for alcohol- and drug-related issues almost half a dozen times at this point.

"I'm a survivor."

"Tell me about that."

"I know I'm going to be okay. I'm using what's come my way to get strong. I don't have anybody to blame for sitting in this shithole. It's all on me. After I leave this jail, I got two more stops where I'll have to do time. But eventually I'll get out and then the tough stuff happens. Alcohol and drugs all the hell over the place, and all my friends wanting me to join them at the bar."

"Whew," I said. "That's the hard part for sure."

"I'm going to survive that too."

Nat was so young, but anyone could see he had personal power. To some degree that was true of all the men in our group tonight. Yet I felt as though we were offering needed reminders to one another. With Jess, perhaps, it was more something on his wish list than an actual outlook; he was still learning about his sense of self, as reflected by others. But listening to the men tonight, I believed a seed was being planted for him.

And me? I held personal power now. But I hadn't always. Neither had I always remembered that I held it. It had taken me most of my life to acknowledge my inner strength. I had used it wrongly for so long. I used it to feel that I could let people walk all over me and I'd somehow come out all right. I still did that. Where did this twisted use of my confidence and perseverance come from? To rehash an old Ricky Nelson song, my bucket had a hole in it. A lack of self-worth or some mangled idea of turning the other cheek set me up. Though all along I had believed I was a survivor, I acted at times like a victim.

For one thing, it seemed I had always felt happier than others — not in a manic way but rather in holding a sturdy ground of quiet, inner joy. I sensed a kind of "bounce-ability" in myself that I didn't detect in those I had allowed to mow over me. Yet I also suspected that I didn't like conflict and that my confidence didn't extend into the areas of defending myself from the kinds of vague, inconspicuous, imperceptible hurts that do me in the most. Such covert issues allowed me too much room to disbelieve my experience. Instead of addressing such encounters, I mended myself and moved on, sometimes setting myself back onto the path of being harmed once more, in the same old way, from the same old person.

This was the trouble with the workshops. Not only did I wrestle with how the inmates suffered and how well or poorly I met that, but my own stuff was stirred up and rose to the surface. I might as well cross sleep off the calendar for Tuesday nights.

Again I realized that I taught what I needed to know. Tonight I was teaching personal power. Survivor versus victim energy. It brought to mind a friend. Though Dana and I had known each other for thirty years, I had not let myself see her dismissiveness. Many warm and happy events were mixed in there to throw me off, if I wanted to be thrown off. But three decades was a long time to let a growing pile of slights go by. It even felt a bit embarrassing to finally want to respond to this imbalance in our old friendship. And yet as I drove home from the detention center in the icy winter night, I could not erase what I had just come to know. And so, puzzling as it may be to her, and as reluctant as I was, I knew that it was time to act on this awareness.

I had allowed mild forms of disrespect to occur in my relationship with Dana, and I kept showing up for more. The fact that a string of small inconsiderate acts and unspoken messages announced that I was further down on her list of friends while Dana resided near the top of mine was something I had not addressed, or refused to acknowledge, or kept excusing. I believed I carried an odd sense of superiority — that of being able to withstand someone's devaluing without feeling devalued. I now saw that I had been fooling myself.

I skidded into a turn toward home, felt my rear tires swim briefly across the ice before correcting. Dana and I had made plans to cross-country ski together on Friday. On Thursday I texted to see what time we should meet in the park. She texted back that she was traveling in Montana and that she couldn't possibly meet me. And I let that go, said not one word in my defense. I would be running into Dana again around town and again she would say, "Let's get together, I mean it. This Saturday. I'll call you."

What would I say? I tested a response in my imagination as I carefully braked on the glaring white road for a stop sign: "No, it's my turn, Dana, not to call you."

I remembered that once you acknowledged something you'd like to change and became fully conscious of it, a change already had begun. Often all that was required was that you went with it. Perhaps I had just taken a step toward valuing myself. But it might help if I tacked this quote from Maya Angelou onto my mirror: "Never make someone a priority when all you are to them is an option."

Actually, my issue with Dana was a remnant of how I had devalued myself throughout the early decades of my marriage. My former husband was an artist who excelled in many areas.

He painted, sculpted in welded metal, made prints — he won a National Endowment of the Arts fellowship for his serigraphs — created beautiful gold and silver jewelry, acted in community theater, directed plays, could pick up a random musical instrument and play a song on it, and his singing voice was so uniquely stirring, it could bring tears to my eyes.

My joke was that I had two skills. I could type and birth babies, and he was to keep strictly away from performing either of them. What I didn't say was how strongly I yearned to use that typing skill to write creatively. But my job, as I saw it then, was being the support team for my husband's art career. During the years when his career went well, I didn't want to detract from his success. During the years when he had trouble producing his art, it felt inappropriate for me to inject myself as a creative person.

It was entirely my own doing, making my sense of my creative fulfillment not a priority but merely an option.

Oddly, it might have been my sense of the unlikeliness of my success that opened the door for me to begin writing my first novel. Because one day I just decided: I am going to do this. I am going to write. But I also decided to keep it a secret.

I hadn't been tested in the ways the inmates had, hadn't been deliberately devalued as a form of punishment, as the inmates experienced repeatedly. What I wanted the guys to know tonight, and what I needed to remember myself, was that ultimately we held the authority over our own sense of value.

I pulled into my neighborhood and spotted the nearly full moon riding the crest of Snow King Mountain, rising through the pines at the very top, outlining each of them like a chiseled print. I thought to myself, We'll need — or at least, I'll need — another Tuesday-night session discussing personal power. Because I felt some seismic prospecting was in order for me. My awareness of how I had allowed myself to be devalued and dismissed had let me know how unstable was the ground of my self-esteem. How two opposing plates were creating a dangerous fault line in my foundation.

# [ Chapter Eleven ]

I used to think that I'd had no experience with inmates until I began the journaling workshops, but that was because I'd forgotten my weekend entertainment as a teenager. I was fifteen, bored, and a bit resentful about babysitting my four-year-old little sister every Friday night while my parents went out. Once I got Gigi into bed and asleep, I had the rest of the evening to myself. I could look through my mom's underwear drawer, where she kept her special things, and try to find proof that I was adopted. That would explain why I had to suffer like Cinderella on a Friday night when all my friends were out ice-skating. Or I could call in to the radio station.

Word had gotten around that if you phoned into the request line at a certain radio station on weekend nights, the station that played the music my friends and I in Cincinnati loved most, the line would invariably be busy. And that was a good thing. The deal was, you had to say your telephone number, number by number, in between the busy signals. So buzz — 2 — buzz — 8 — buzz — and so on. I wasn't sure I believed the rumor about somebody hearing your number and calling you. Still, I'd already sneaked peeks at my mom's novel *Peyton Place*, which the adults were talking about in hushed tones, and which

I'd found tucked beneath her folded sweaters, so I gave calling the radio station a try.

Snow fell past the dark kitchen window above the sink while I leaned against the doorjamb leading to the dining room and gave out my number in between buzzes of the busy signal. Then I hung up the phone and began to look for the hidden bottles of Coca-Cola in the refrigerator. My mother kept Coke on hand for her lunches but not for my pleasure. If there were more than two bottles, I could likely sneak one undetected.

The phone rang.

"Hello?" Decades later I still slapped myself once in a while when answering the phone with a tentative question in my voice, as if I was scared someone were actually on the other end of the line.

"Hi," answered the voice of a strange boy.

Uh-oh, I thought and, looking down at the outgrown pajamas I was wearing, ridiculously wishing I was dressed better.

"Hi," I said. Softer and surer this time, going for mysterious woman possibly wearing a negligee.

"Got your number from the radio station." To this day, I don't know how or why this worked, but the teenagers in Cincinnati had figured it out. "My name is Kenny. What's yours?"

Thus began a year-long phone friendship. Kenny called every Friday night. Eventually I picked up some information about him, but he was guarded. I was too naive to be guarded, so he knew far more about me than I knew about him, and this could have been dangerous for me, but it wasn't.

Not, as it turned out, until Kenny got sent to jail and wrote me from there with the return address on the envelope (as the law required) — and my parents plucked it out of the mailbox. Then I was grounded for the usual month. They got a free babysitter both Friday *and* Saturday night that way. I spent half my teen years grounded for the merest infractions of the rules: Home two minutes after the 11:30 curfew on Saturday nights, sassing my mother, a C+ on my report card, not cleaning my room before the cleaning lady showed. A month each time. Looking back, this could have been wise parenting on their part. I missed many unsupervised parties with illegally purchased liquor and sleepovers with my girlfriends who stole their parents' cars late at night and drove around town in their pajamas. And when I was allowed out on Saturday night, I had to be home, standing under the porch light, before most of the real fun happened. Since my father flicked the porchlight repeatedly at 11:30 on the dot, there wasn't any goodnight kissing either.

I don't know what Kenny was arrested for. I never got to see his letter and had to vow never to connect with him again. But in the meantime, before his arrest, we had nice long Friday-evening conversations. Once I was on Bob Braun's Saturday afternoon dance show, a Cincinnati version of Dick Clark's show. In between couples free dancing to popular records, there were performances by high school kids. That Saturday afternoon the performance was by my modern jazz dance class. After we danced to "PEnnsylvania 6-5000," Bob Braun pulled me out of the group, asked my name, and raved about my long eyelashes. Had me stand sideways and told the cameraman to zoom in. Kenny was watching the show. So now he knew a *lot* more about me than I did him.

Kenny told me that his sister Babs had been watching the show too and informed him I was way out of his league. Too good for him, and he should stick with girls he had a chance with. But we weren't in a romance, not even flirty with each other. We liked to talk. Or was that my naivety again?

I wasn't surprised to receive a letter sent by Kenny from jail; I knew he'd been arrested before. What I had gathered was that he was a couple years older than me, lived in the poor or more likely very poor part of the city, hadn't finished high school, was a nice guy, and never went over the line of friendship with me. Not once.

When I didn't answer Kenny's letter, I never heard from him again.

It was odd to think that my brief friendship with Kenny foreshadowed the jail workshops that became a focus of my life fifty years later.

Now I realized that Kenny probably never assumed anything could happen beyond our Friday-night phone calls, because likely he harbored the same low self-esteem as did so many of the inmates I had encountered over the years. In fact, an entire section of my notebook, with quotes and journaling questions, was titled "Self-Esteem." As a rule the inmates didn't think too well of themselves. They had felt unworthy through much of their lives and, of course, especially during their incarceration.

I wanted the men who came to the journaling workshop to know that dignity resided in a place where no person or circumstance could rob them of it. And that was a challenge when, following our workshop, each man would endure a body search before being led back to his cell. And yet there was no better time to learn that you were not the victim you were treated as. If the inmates could acquire a sense of self-worth under such circumstances, I imagined they could own it almost unchallenged for the rest of their lives.

# [ Chapter Twelve ]

"What do you want me to do with this?" Phillip asked me and nodded to the journal I'd passed to an officer to give him.

Phillip looked to be in his late thirties, healthy, strong, very attentive, and nicely mannered. Called me ma'am. But I saw something behind those hazel eyes. Chaotic mind spins, I suspected, that kept his thoughts circling like hungry coyotes around an injured elk. He came down to meet with me alone from being locked up in a maximum-security cell. He was still locked up, but so was I, since we each sat in a separate locked-down room divided by a grate.

I told him that the journal was his, adding that no one in my seven years had ever had a journal taken away from them or read by anyone. "However," I said, "don't incriminate yourself." I explained that journaling was all about the inner life — thoughts, emotions, memories, dreams, fears, and hopes. I said, "Write about that."

I suggested we do a quick exercise, my old standby for when I had no clues yet about what an inmate needed. "Name three people you admire and enjoy. They can be real people or movie or book characters, dead or alive, family members or strangers."

Next I asked him to write down the qualities he admired about these people. I gave him a few minutes, and then I asked about his list. "Did you come up with three people?"

Phillip said, "Yes, ma'am. I put down my uncle, my older brother, and my grandfather."

"And what did you put down for the characteristics you admire in them?"

Phillip read from his journal. "Honesty, trustworthiness, hardworking, fun to be around, kind, intelligent, interesting, real likable. Ma'am."

I said, "All those qualities belong to you too, Phillip, or at least the potential for them, the seed of them, otherwise you wouldn't be able to recognize them in others."

He looked stunned.

His eyes glistened.

Then a faint smile. Then the smile grew bigger and Phillip got excited. He dropped the "yes, ma'ams."

"Dude, you don't know what you just did for me. Dude, you don't know what you just said. Aw, dude."

He blinked back tears.

I blinked back mine.

"I talk shit to myself. I'm up there in that crummy cell all alone and I tell myself what a piece of crap I am and I just want to... you know."

I didn't know. But after he told me his older brother was his idol and that he had committed suicide this past year, I guessed I did know. But this moment felt as if a skinny beam of light was shining into deep darkness.

I assigned Phillip homework. "This week fill a couple of pages in your journal with a list of your good qualities. And then you'll have this to remind yourself."

Our time was up.

Why were we all so hard on ourselves, so quick to absorb blame, feel shame, head for the lowest possible judgment of ourselves? I was guilty of this. The first hint of an edgy relationship, and I'm all over myself like ants on a picnic crumb, devouring my actions and words, finding fault in both. I used the harshest language on myself, set higher standards for my actions than for anyone else's. It could take a long time of self-recrimination for me to realize who I was at heart, to revive trust in my worthiness.

I like to tell the inmates a story I heard from my meditation teacher about a time when the Dalai Lama met with a large group of American Buddhist teachers who had gathered in Dharamsala, India.

The Dalai Lama asked, "What is the biggest issue for American spiritual seekers?"

The Buddhist teachers said, "Self-esteem."

But the Dalai Lama didn't understand what the term meant.

The Americans tried to translate it for him. After several attempts to explain, one teacher said, "They don't love themselves."

And the Dalai Lama cried.

# [ Chapter Thirteen ]

One Tuesday night the inmates and I talked about being present to what life offered in the moment. A difficult subject when you felt life wasn't really going to begin until you were released from jail. The prevailing attitude was that time locked up was time to be ticked off day by day and endured. Many inmates endured by flattening emotionally, expecting nothing, feeling aroused by nothing. Some went from marker to marker: night of sleep to night of sleep, meal to meal, weekend to weekend, when visiting hours are scheduled.

Jody said, "Hey, it's Tuesday night to Tuesday night. You're the only thing happening here."

But Jody had no family nearby to visit him, and because he was arrested for domestic battery shortly after moving here with his girlfriend, he had no local friends. So Tuesdays probably starred as his Saturday night on the town. But it was true that there were no other interactions with the local community, no classes or other workshops offered. AA meetings occurred erratically, and sometimes a church service.

Tonight we were deep into winter in our mountain valley, snow piled high, temperatures dropped low. I wore knee-high boots with thick ice-grabbing soles. Trudging through the unplowed snow to and from my car meant sinking into the icy stuff over the top of my boots, and now I felt it melt and trickle inside to dampen my socks. My hooded down coat and puffy mittens were starred with snowflakes. A shortage of officers tonight relegated the workshop to the grated lockdown. Four men sat crammed together on one side of the metal grate, waiting for me. And though I felt my usual flash of claustrophobia when the door on my side clanged shut and locked, I had enough room to flap out of my coat and drape it over the extra chair.

Our small group consisted of guys who had been attending the workshop since autumn: Brodie, Colt, and Jody, with one man, Anton, who we were all familiar with from his two previous incarcerations that winter. Since I had an unusually long relationship with all four of the men, it was a good time to go a bit deeper into a stickier topic.

I said, "This isn't going to be your favorite subject, but here's a quote from Eckhart Tolle I'd like us to work with tonight." I read the quote out loud from an index card: "Whatever the present moment contains, accept it as if you have chosen it."

I went on. "You live locked down, with minimal choices, suited in stripes, eating bland foods, and I'm suggesting you look at the situation as if you have chosen this for yourself." I had some nerve saying this to the men. But I knew these guys well enough to admire their range of thought, and I really wanted to place this piece in our discussion. I said, "Perhaps you chose it for a kind of healing or passage toward wholeness or perhaps to save yourself from further harm."

I paused, then continued, "Some wisdom teachers hold that we have a spirit spark within and that it will fight to keep itself alive for you, no matter what it has to bring into your life. That this spirit spark will ultimately guide you toward whatever it takes to keep itself blazing within you. We humans often will only be halted in our pursuit of distraction by the harshest of situations — illness, injury... incarceration."

The men were listening. They sat in silence, no knee bouncing, no pencil drumming.

"Is this ridiculous? Or can you imagine incarceration possibly being something you unconsciously brought to yourself? Perhaps as a way of moving deeper into life, or maybe as a form of survival."

Colt responded right away, "If I hadn't gotten arrested I'd be dead by now. I'm not joking. I needed to be stopped." At age twenty-three, Colt had been arrested six times for drinking while driving or for public intoxication. He nodded, "So, yeah, I guess I saved myself by picking a fight with that cop."

Anton said, "That cop picked a fight with *me*. Or I'd still be out there having a good time." Anton wasn't there yet, but I have come to enjoy his spirit. He reminded me of my pup Emmett who hears me call "come," and before responding looks around to see if something else might be more interesting. Since this was Anton's third arrest in a few months, I imagined that instead of following the rules of his probation he'd found something else more interesting.

Colt grinned and nodded toward Anton. "That was me a couple of arrests back."

Jody too felt set up, in his case by his old girlfriend, but was making the best of his incarceration by learning about law and helping the other guys organize their defenses. But he agreed in part. "I didn't know I enjoyed law as much as I do. I like helping these guys through the legal maze."

Brodie sat, looking thoughtful. I raised my eyebrows in question at him.

He spoke thoughtfully. "My wife said I should consider that I am living in retreat, with time alone to think about life and the opportunity to grow spiritually. So I am drawing a lot, reading, and thinking about my life. She's right. I need this."

We had talked before about Joseph Campbell's belly of the whale segment of the hero's journey. So I liked that Brodie was using this time to go inward.

I said, "To accept the idea of choosing the situation, we can consider each other as our current family. This is who we are living in relationship with right now. Who we are interacting with, who we are testing our ethics and our value systems with."

I took a big breath before announcing the particularly galling aspect of this idea. "This family includes the officers." Because these guys acted politely around me, they were holding their reactions until I asked for them, which I planned on doing, but not just yet.

"What if," I asked, "we acted as if we had chosen the people around us as well as the circumstances? For one thing, we couldn't seek refuge in victimhood or feel angry at others about our fate. We'd have to claim our situation. We'd have to view one another as our family or community, sharing what life presented. To resist or deny life as it is now is useless." I took a shallow breath. "Also, kind of... deranged."

I'd just announced to these dear men who were locked up and ruled by armed guards that they were deranged if they didn't think of their guards as family members.

I had in mind another quote, this one by Maya Angelou. I read it out loud. "You may not control all the events that happen to you, but you can decide not to be reduced by them."

Jody said, "Exactly."

All four men asked me to repeat the quote so they could copy it into their journals.

"Just for the heck of it, this coming week, practice opening your mind to this place as your home *for now* and to the people here as your family or community *for now*."

Some of their expressions suggested I'd gone too far.

Even so, I pushed it a bit more. "Because if you can accomplish this, even briefly, here in jail, you may experience a life of feeling comfortable wherever you are and whoever you're with."

I checked out each of the four men; all of them had their eyes latched onto mine. Possibly feeling incredulous that I'd say such a thing. So I asked, "Does this sound absurd to you?"

Brodie said, "I guess I could try thinking about living with a different family for a while." He added, "But I would not want my wife and daughter or my mother and little brothers to live like this, ever." Brodie shook his head. "It's too hard."

"How about you, Colt?"

Colt gave a sarcastic laugh. He said, "Not absurd, but I can't help thinking there are two opposing sides in here: us and them. Inmates and officers. Because that's just the way it's set up. You can't ignore it." He shook his head. "The officers don't let you."

Jody said, "They like it that way; they've got the power."

Anton said, "Yeah, and they push it in our faces every chance they get. Even in the middle of the night when we're trying to sleep. Every hour, they slam each cell door hard during their night check. Each metal slam resounds all over the place, upstairs and down. They don't have to slam those doors. It's like some kind of torture to be jerked out of sleep every hour."

I nodded in understanding. I got it. Incarceration was *tough*. It was difficult to imagine there were jail officers who thought it wasn't already tough enough.

Colt said, "There's nothing we can do, even if we wanted to make it friendlier around here."

"One thing you've got," I said, "is the way you look out of

your eyes." I saw recognition in the men's sly smiles. Their eyes were the inmates' only weapons here. "I suspect you all harden them to send a message." Nods around the group, with bigger smiles.

"Try softening your eyes."

Then I asked, "Has anybody had family members while growing up or others in your adult life who made you feel the way the officers make you feel?"

A spill of stories tumbled out from each of the four about a bullying older brother, a raging father, cruel foster parents, teachers that dismissed their intelligence. Time after time these men had been kicked while down, their selfhood crushed.

This was what I was getting at. I said, "What you are saying is that this pattern has appeared in your lives before." I hadn't met an inmate yet who didn't have someone in their childhood with power over them who abused the situation. I said, "As an experiment, instead of repeating your same old response, try a different tack with this 'us and them' setup. Go into it in a way you haven't tried before. When you change, everything around has to shift at least a little bit in order to adjust." I'm hoping that at a minimum one of them will gain a stronger sense of personal power and find new dignity in this response. But I don't deal in outcomes.

The mood felt heavy and dark, so I said, "The officers are part of your family. However, if you accidentally call Officer Bryant 'uncle' I take no responsibility."

The guys laughed.

A guard peered into the sliver of window in the metal door, and then unlocked it. The men pushed back their chairs and lined up to leave.

"Remember," I said, "you're a valuable family member. Stand tall. With soft eyes."

I decided right then that I wouldn't ask next week how the experiment went. The inmates' circumstances made this a difficult challenge. I felt urged to bring the idea into our workshop, but I knew from my own experience that it could take years and a hundred attempts to pull off a sense of self-regard while faced with another's disdain.

# [ Chapter Fourteen ]

Bart was a Native American from the Shoshone tribe, stocky, with a kind face and quiet manner. He was arrested for driving a busload of assisted-living residents across Wyoming on a field trip while being inebriated. It wasn't his first DUI, and he was sentenced to a full year in the Teton County Jail.

In our journaling workshop Bart answered every journaling prompt with the same two words: *My family.*

Head down, he'd mumble those two words each time in answer to all five questions week after week, month after month.

What makes you happiest?

My family.

What makes you saddest?

My family.

If I asked for more information, Bart would mumble, "I don't know. Just family."

"Who is in your family, Bart?"

"Aunts."

"Anyone else?"

"Some kids."

"Who in your family do you feel closest to?"

"My grandfather."

Ah, now I've got something to work with. I perked up, expectant. "Tell me about him."

"He's dead."

Hmm. Still, I thought, maybe we could get somewhere with this. I asked if his grandfather had gone on a vision quest. He had, but Bart didn't remember much that he was told about it; his grandfather had died when he was young. So in Bart's honor, I led the group into a simulated vision quest, checking with Bart all the way to see what further information he might offer, but he kept his head down.

For the version I created I asked the guys three questions. The first was to write about a person living or dead that they thought of as being wise or a mentor or in any way helpful, along with a few lines about that person and their helpfulness.

Bart put down one word. *Grandfather*.

Next I asked the men to write down one question they would ask this person about their life and what that person might say in return. I suggested they ask something that could be helpful to them upon leaving jail and returning to their regular lives.

Bart responded with his usual answer. He wrote *family*.

And finally, the third piece was to write down an animal that was meaningful to them. Afterward I looked up the meanings of each animal in my medicine card book and read it out loud. This was the men's favorite part. They took the symbolism to heart and liked hearing the positive qualities attached to their choices. It was my favorite part too. It felt like it was a way to tell them with an extra dose of authority about their inner value.

Here Bart left his paper blank.

"When you walk outside your home, what creature are you likely to notice first?"

Bart shrugged. "A hawk in the sky, I guess."

I looked up *hawk* and read snippets of description about hawk energy. "When hawk energy belongs to you, it tells you to pay attention to everything around you and how you feel inside your body."

The idea was for the men to have an exercise in personal inquiry in a brief and simple form. A small insight or intention pinned down in words, along with two figures to support carrying through on it.

Another inmate also wrote down *grandfather*, and the question he asked was how could he hold down a job to take care of his family while also getting some schooling. He imagined this answer from his grandfather, who had died a few years earlier: "It will take longer than you want, but you can do it. Just start." The animal the man chose was elk. The message about elk energy was about stamina and pacing oneself. Elk people weren't always the first to meet their goal, but they got there.

Family. That was all I continued to get from Bart, and yet he came down to the workshop every single Tuesday night, never missed a week for eleven months.

And then one night he burst out with several long sentences.

"Thank you for coming every week and asking questions. I think better now. I didn't know before about stuff, you know, like organizing my thoughts." Without pausing, he continued to look straight at me and said, "I went to court and I could say things to the judge. I told him I had changed a lot and I am writing things in the notebook you gave me. So thank you."

He added, "I'm being released early."

It turned out that Bart was given early release for good behavior and for being an inmate worker, doing laundry and helping in the kitchen. I don't know why it took nearly a year for Bart to put his words together and to look directly at me long enough to say them all, but I could have puddled into a weepy mess, I was so pleased for him and his ability to become conscious of himself.

Maybe it wasn't so unusual that it took Bart eleven months to talk to me in full sentences, since it took me an awfully long time to put words to and make sense of what I experienced too. In fact, it has always been one of my embarrassments that I was slow in that way. I came from a family that was whip smart, fast with retorts, funny as hell, and loved to banter, which just highlighted my slower ways.

Along with a love for family, Bart and I shared these slower ways.

# [ Chapter Fifteen ]

I heard a story once about a man who kept changing the temperature controls in the house he shared with his wife. When she remarked that she was chilled or overheated, he told her she was crazy to think that, that he was fine, that nothing was different. He worked at getting her to disbelieve herself.

This story resonated with me. For years, because of my ability to empathize with others, I valued their perspectives more than my own experience. Little did I realize that I had somehow jumped over the toddler stage of selfishness, only to have to reenter it in my late forties. I had to learn to be selfish. And then, of course, I took it too far.

My love of writing coincided with that time and opened up a locked box that spilled with an urgency to gather all my toys to myself and say no a lot. After spending many adult years making sure my husband and sons got what they needed and wanted, it was the first time I had wanted something just for myself. So I overreacted in trying to get time and space to do what I loved most, and halted many exchanges with people abruptly. It created puzzlement and confusion and a fair bit of anger toward me. I stopped drunken phone calls late at night from a beloved old friend. I gave my husband's family back to him — no more relaying phone messages from his mother or anguishing over gifts for his father. I scooted away from the dinner table the first moment I could and stopped spending the evenings watching TV with my husband and sons. I postponed a visit from my mother. All to buy time to write. I balanced out eventually, but it was jarring for everyone to have a people pleaser depart and be replaced with a self-centered two-year-old.

Once when my mother was deep into Alzheimer's, I contacted my Aunt Iva to check up on some vague memories I carried from my toddler years. Both my mother and aunt lived with my grandparents while their husbands were in the army, and so Iva was present during that time of my life.

I asked my aunt, "I seem to have a memory of my mother asking me for my opinions and decisions as early as when I was three years old. But that sounds so preposterous that I wanted to check with you."

Aunt Iva said, "Oh, yes. Why, I said to Pop, your grandfather, Alice sure leans on that little girl."

My aunt confirmed my memories of being asked to participate fully in my mother's life, such as where we should go, if we should go, and when. I also recall my mother's fear when people on the bus would talk to me. I've seen a picture of myself at three: dimpled knees poking out of my red wool coat with chubby cheeks below the matching red wool hat. People liked to talk to cute kids on the bus and in shops, but when that happened my mother would pinch my arm and lean down to whisper fiercely into my ear, "Don't talk to that lady." Then a minute later, "Stop smiling at her." I was taught to be empathic by my mother in order to meet her needs, and yet she demanded that I not respond to someone complimenting me on my shiny patent-leather shoes or nice blue eyes.

Since my admirer assumed I was just acting shy, she would smile wider, bend closer to me, and repeat her kind words, while my mother squeezed the soft bones of my hand to the point of numbness and radiated anger at me. My mother wasn't strong enough herself to walk the two of us away or ask the person to leave us alone. She required me to relay the message for her. As a three-year-old I tried to oblige her, but the job of withstanding the tug-of-war between my mother and the threatening world she lived in left me feeling inadequate. Such friendly encounters with the larger world felt right, but according to my mother they were wrong.

Once we got off the bus or out of the shop with the worrisomely friendly lady, my mother would yank me down the street by my red-coated arm, ranting furiously at me about my shortcomings in minding her.

And so I grew to be a woman who did not believe her own experience. That is, it was hard to do so without some self-training, in which I was still engaged.

The first few years of my life, my father was not living with us but rather visited, while being shipped here and there during his time in the army. My father returned, my brother was born, and I sensed that I was released from the full responsibility of my mother. But by then you could have told me snow was not chilly when held against the skin of my tummy, and I would have nodded in agreement. I was out there, residing in other peoples' minds and bodies. Checking everyone's face for clues as to how I should feel, what I should think. I'm still pretty good at that. The trick has been not to discard that habit but to turn that way of being into a skill that serves me and others. In the meantime, I often found it safest to try to please everyone.

• • • •

One Tuesday night I asked the inmates, "Is it difficult for you to say no?" The answer was surprisingly consistent: Yes. Each of them struggled with saying no. I doubted it was common knowledge that the incarcerated have a tendency to be nice guys, but that was my experience.

Randy was a good example.

I had been seeing Randy for eight and half months of Tuesday nights. He was in his midthirties, a man of slight build sporting a wispy goatee, an on-again, off-again addict, and according to his own description, fairly undirected in his life. He was arrested because he gave a powerful painkiller that he'd been prescribed for his back pain to a woman who told him she was in dire agony from her own back pain.

Randy said, "I knew just how she felt. I had a few remaining pills from a prescription, so I gave them to her." He did this even knowing he couldn't get the prescription refilled. That was how nice he was. The woman, in her early forties, died shortly after. About the same time Randy was arrested for possession of illegal drugs. Somehow the two incidents — his arrest and the woman's death — were linked, and Randy was charged with a long list of possible crimes in order to keep him incarcerated until the woman's cause of death was determined. All the while, he was being referred to as an alleged murderer by the prosecutor and detectives. It took months before the courts disclosed the autopsy report. Randy learned that she had overdosed herself on alcohol and a collection of drugs, which did not include the pills he had given to her. After months of being threatened with life in prison, Randy was off the hook for a possible murder charge.

It was an occasion for me to do a journaling workshop on the difficulty of saying no, of being a nice guy even when it went against your own well-being. I was talking to myself the whole time.

Randy said, "Yeah. I shouldn't have done it. I didn't really know that woman. But I know how bad that pain is. Still, I want people to like me too much sometimes, so I do what people want me to do, even if I really don't want to do it."

He spoke for the group. We all nodded vigorously.

Often Randy would recruit new inmates to our workshop, and I could discern what he'd told the first-timer to expect. I'd do one of my cheerleading sis-boom-bah talks and catch Randy exchanging glances and a secret smile with the new guy, and I'd know that he'd told them something about me and my pep rallies. Or I'd hold up an index card, about to read a quote that fit our workshop subject, and Randy would nod knowingly at his cellmate, as in: "See, I told you she'd do that."

Randy often copied into his journal the quotes of wisdom teachers that I read to the group. I especially liked that since it seemed like evidence that I'd hit a receptive place. And yet I never felt that Randy soaked up the insights. Each week we seemed to begin at step one. That notion was confirmed a year and half later. Randy had been sent to additional incarceration in a state prison and then to a halfway house. There he worked steadily at a job, stayed clean, and was released. Within a couple of days he was arrested again for possession of illegal drugs.

So now he was back in the Teton County Detention Center, and we enjoyed a nice reunion, despite the oddness of that occurring in jail. A week later he said to me, "Well, I found out how I got arrested again. My ex-wife, you know, the mother of my little boy, called the cops from Vermont and told them I had drugs on me." He sneered and shook his head in disgust that the mother of Charlie, his three-year-old, would do that when she was thousands of miles away and hadn't had any contact with him whatsoever.

I said, "I'm sorry to hear that."

"Yeah," Randy said. "She didn't even know. She just guessed and got me arrested again."

I said, "Hmm. She was right too."

He dipped his head and grinned sheepishly, like this was him being naughty, not him heading to prison another time. So much for the talk about the fishing he and his son would do together, the career in computers, the nice house with a yard for his little boy to play in. But it was difficult for me to be more than momentarily annoyed with Randy. He was such a nice guy.

One of the things Randy used to lure newcomers to our workshop was our game of chance with my set of spirit animal cards. Tonight we were all crammed into the grated room. Me, alone on one side of the metal grate, five inmates sitting in plastic chairs, elbow to elbow, on the other side. They were so crowded into the tiny space that an inmate had to stand and hold his chair up over his head if an officer needed to open the door.

The vent on my side of the room blasted either icy air or stuffy hot air, but I couldn't complain since I had four times more breathing space than the men did. Still, I owned throw rugs bigger than my side of the room, and each time that metal door clanged shut, I had to tamp down a rising desire to scream for help. Tonight the vent was huffing out cold air, and I wanted to reach for my coat, but the inmates were wearing short-sleeved shirts and were even more uncomfortable. I decided to tough it out.

"Let's see what chance has to tell you tonight."

I fanned the animal spirit cards out in my hands and held the cards facedown toward the grate. Each inmate scooted up close to the grate and studied the backs of the cards, then pointed to the card they wanted. They took this part seriously. I pulled the card out and wedged it into the small glass window framed into the grate. Once all five guys had their cards, I waited for those who liked to copy down the message, then they took turns reading their message out loud, and I supplemented by reading the information provided in the accompanying booklet. We were happily amazed at how often the message on the spirit animal card matched the issues a particular inmate had earlier discussed.

Tonight Randy drew the polar bear card. "Stand up for yourself and speak your truth respectfully and compassionately, with no attachment to outcome." He copied it down. I read a few lines from the booklet that discussed setting boundaries.

Both Randy and I needed that polar bear card.

# [ Chapter Sixteen ]

I'm convinced that we experience more than one belly of the whale stage in our lives. Times of abrupt change or sudden lulls, when events or the lack of them, drive us inward. The five years I spent in Cheyenne before moving to Jackson Hole come to mind.

It was a time of limbo. After a few exhilarating years of working at an alternative Cincinnati area radio station, my then husband and I decided to move our family to a place so alien to me that I had to learn the language. How come *one animal unit* was really two animals, a cow and calf? *Whiteout* had a whole different meaning than the fluid I used typing, which I learned while dangerously driving in one.

I remembered sitting in the small sunroom of our tiny house beneath huge cottonwoods, looking out the window, and wondering why nothing was moving for me. Why there were so few stimuli in my life. Yet now I looked back on that time and recognized the major changes that occurred outside my awareness. For the first time, after years of dreaming, I took my longing to write seriously and spent my days, while my sons were in school, writing in that little sunroom. I had borrowed a portable typewriter from my husband's office and set it on top of a small wooden apple crate, pulled up a child's footstool, and with my knees up by my chin, typed until I saw the school bus pull up.

Before unpacking the moving boxes in Cheyenne, I met a woman who became a spiritual teacher for me and my new friend Eve. For five years she and I drove the hundred-and-fifty-mile round trip each week to meet with Genie, our teacher, for three hours, sometimes needing to bring our little boys along, a rowdy gang of four. This laid a pathway for the following decades' study of philosophy.

It was also a time when I fell deeply in love with the outdoors. I bought my first pair of hiking boots and felt powerful in them. I spent my weekdays writing and the weekends with my family driving an hour to Vedauwoo, where we hiked. Usually straight up. The sandstone mountains grabbed my thick treads and let me walk in places that made my heart thud fast and swell in awe. Along narrow edges, looking down on steep drops, teetering on nearly perpendicular walls to reach a pointy overlook. I was amazed at myself and the wild beauty of the world. It felt as though it was the boots, those heavy, thick-leathered, deeply treaded hiking boots that opened my world and gave me courage.

Charles Levendosky was Wyoming's poet laureate, and he welcomed me as a writer within our first weeks of unloading the moving truck. This kind welcome was based on nothing but hearing from someone that I *wanted* to write. I began writing poems, partly because of Charles, partly because poems were short. I could write swiftly and just as swiftly pull my pen back in a kind of shock, my hands raised as if touching something hot. I took a class Charles taught. The night we had to read our work out loud to the group, I wore those big clunky hiking boots and felt courageous enough in them to stand up and meet the assignment.

Three things were established for me during that belly of the whale period: I began a lifetime spiritual practice, I wrote seriously, and I became a lover of the natural world. These three are the pillars of my life now. But back then, like many of the inmates who attended the jail workshop, I didn't really know myself, had no idea where I was going or what I found meaningful in life.

During that time I began to break away just a bit from the mindset of the dependent wife. Though most of the time I didn't believe what I began to notice. I pushed aside the quiet voice suggesting that I not follow along on everything my husband dreamed up. He was so good at dreaming things up; it's very much why I was attracted to him in the first place. With this guy, I thought, I will not have a traditional life. I will live a creative life filled with unique experiences. The fact that our first son was born exactly to the day ten months after our wedding diverted that thinking somewhat. But I so loved being a mother that next on my to-do list was not traveling with a backpack — the life I had envisioned — but having another baby. Which I promptly accomplished.

Yet true to my original vision, three years after the birth of our second son, my husband and I sold everything we owned, bought a camper van, and headed off into the world for a year of travel, toddlers in tow. We didn't realize at the time, or for many months after, that the nomadic life had become a hippie tradition on the West Coast. In the East we were seen as a clean-cut family giving ourselves a unique experience, an extended vacation (involving occasional jobs). Once we arrived in the West, we were part of a movement.

After returning home we resumed a traditional life that veered off only for moves to more interesting places for jobs or schooling. And then Jackson Hole came along, and life soared for me. We opened a resort shop, which was pretty adventuresome for me, considering how little I knew about retailing. I invented my own ledger system before discovering the exact same thing in the office supply store. That experience informed me how unprepared I was to run a resort shop and also handed me the confidence I needed — if I could independently create the ledger the standard business world used, maybe I did know how to run a shop. After a few years of managing the business, I was comfortable enough with its demands to devote myself to writing seriously again.

Imagination played a large role all along, even when I attributed my courage to my new hiking boots. I imagined how to be a mother, a shop owner and bookkeeper, a writer, a woman hiking alone up canyons in the Tetons, all before I actually acted on any of it.

Imagination was a mentor for me. Leading the workshops on Tuesday nights had shown me how valuable imagination is to our lives. For the men who struggled with addiction, imagining themselves leading a life without drugs or alcohol was a major step toward their sobriety. Imagining who they wished to become upon release was a valuable use of their time in isolation.

I was astounded the first time an inmate said, "What do you mean by the word *imagination*?" I felt like someone was asking me what I meant by walking, sitting, breathing. I was stymied for a moment, then I began with the basics.

"Every time you eat, you have to first picture the fork going from the food on your plate to your mouth."

I got a slow nod from Rafe, who'd asked the question

during a one-on-one meeting while he was in maximum security. Rafe was arrested for bringing two women to town and covertly advertising them for sexual encounters. A police officer in the line of duty answered the ad. Rafe was a gentle soul who had been stirred by his time in max to wonder a bit about things. He asked me to bring him a list of inspiring quotes that he could study, after I had read a couple of my favorites to him. He had experienced only male role models who had done the same kind of work he had been doing or who sold drugs.

Rafe had a two-year-old daughter with a past girlfriend. One night when he came to meet with me in the grated room, he leaned close in and whispered, "I got this little girl. I started thinking about how I treat girls and I got so broken down this week. I can't have my little girl ever be treated like I do some. I feel sick at what I've done. I got to figure out some other work." He wiped his eyes on the short sleeve of his mustard-yellow top. "I don't know how to do any other work. I got to find some money to feed this girl."

And that was when I suggested he imagine the kind of work he would like to do. But we got stuck on *imagine*. We came up against a wall with every question I asked. Rafe had lived no other way and couldn't picture another way of life.

"Imagination is a skill that can be developed into a valuable tool for our lives," I explained. "If you can imagine... picture... in your mind how you would like to spend a day, you can get closer and closer to designing your day the way you'd like it."

"I get that. Yeah. But I got to have some work. I don't know how to do anything. I don't know what I like to do."

Back to basics. "Do you know how to cook?"

"Yeah, I cook for my family. They like it." He looked as if the memory made him happy.

"There you go. Anybody who can cook can always find people who need feeding. What if you set up a movie in your mind with you standing in a kitchen? People are sitting at a table in the other room, and they are hungry. They are looking forward to seeing what food you will bring them. You grab some eggs and go from there."

Our time was up, according to the officer popping his head through the doorway on Rafe's side of the grate. I said, "Use your journal this week to imagine — picture — what kind of cooking you'd do for those hungry people."

Halfway out the door held open by the officer, Rafe turned to me and said, "It won't be no — what you call them, those fluffy things." Rafe's hand rounded a high mound of something soufflé-like. "But it'll be good."

The officer spoke into his mic, "Charlie Victor 2."

As my door buzzed, I caught it and held it open with the extra chair while I gathered my papers and put on my jacket. Then I shoved the chair aside and let the door fall shut and lock behind me.

• • • •

Outside the slice of a golden moon was headed for the Tetons. It was delicate and tinged with apricot and choked me up to look at it. I got into my car and did the usual: turned the radio on to classical music and drove out of the parking lot, stretching my neck down low to see the moon. Rafe stirred me. Something about his longing and his lack of knowing how or where to direct it. As a person, I found him appealing. His hair was plaited into a bouncing mass of skinny tight braids to his shoulders, with a few that flopped across his features. He was gentle, worried about the two women who were arrested with him, and he was sliced open in a raw and vulnerable way.

I also spent time, separately, with each of the two women. Rebecca, twenty, was an admitted heroin addict and was almost immediately sent to rehab. She was soft-spoken and read some of the poetry she had written during our one meeting. She came down especially to receive a journal so she could write more. The court seemed to find her sympathetic, a victim who would perform sex acts in exchange for the drug she was addicted to. I found the other woman, Brittany, intelligent and strong and maybe a bit in love with Rafe while also aware he wasn't good for her. She and I met every week for several months until her release. She was twenty-two, wore her blonde hair shoulder length, which somewhat concealed a small thorny rose tattoo on the right side of her neck. She sneered when talking about Rebecca and called her a junkie. I suspected she couldn't afford to have much compassion for Rebecca, because if Rebecca had told the authorities that she had been shot up with heroin and taken across state lines, the offenses against both Brittany and Rafe would have been increased manyfold. As it stood, there was little solid evidence against any of them, though according to Brittany the detectives were making her jail time miserable. Constant questioning, threats about increased incarceration, accusations about her withholding evidence, but finally they had to release her.

Now it was Rafe's turn to get the third degree. And the detectives told him that Brittany was released because she had traded her freedom for evidence against him. I knew from the months I spent with Brittany that it wasn't true. Once they could no longer legally keep Rafe in maximum security, they put him in a cell alone for another long series of weeks. Despite this treatment, I heard from other officers that Rafe behaved with quiet decency. He wasn't allowed to join the other men in our group workshop, so I continued to see him separately. He clearly wanted to move beyond his past limits. He was curious and eager to be inspired.

Since I never knew what happened to inmates once they left the county jail, I had to use my imagination to follow them. Once Rebecca was out of rehab, the question loomed whether she would give authorities incriminating information about Rafe and Brittany. My guess was that Rebecca chose not to give out information, or the three of them would have shown up in the Teton County court system once again.

I wondered, did Rebecca clear her addiction to heroin, did she struggle with memories of creepy motel rooms with creepier clients? Did she continue to write poems?

Brittany wanted to attend nursing school. Did she?

How much did Rafe suffer over his past actions? Was he a cook in a café someplace? Did he ever learn to make a soufflé?

# [ Chapter Seventeen ]

One night the guard didn't come to pick up the guys from the grated lockdown until almost twenty minutes past our hour. I'd gotten pretty good at timing the workshop in order to get everything into that hour — the journaling prompts, time to write the responses, time for everyone to talk out loud about their answers. But that night we finished and no one showed up to stop us, so we talked casually, and the subject turned, as it so often did, to drugs and alcohol.

There was a particular pleasure in the day of the life of someone who was high. And much to my horror, it happened to be driving while drunk or on drugs. Music blaring, curvy highways, high speed, drink in hand to top off whatever else had been ingested earlier brought favorite memories and lots of laughter to the guys. This, despite the fact that each one of them sat in a locked-down room across a metal grate from me for that very reason: driving under the influence.

One guy was not laughing. Brodie sat there with only a polite smile. He was facing prison for having killed a man in an accident while driving drunk. After the hilarity calmed, he said, "That's what I did every night after work. I'd buy a six-pack to drive home, maybe have a bottle of tequila in the car close by. Then I'd drive from here to Driggs."

"Oh. My. God," we all exclaimed, practically in unison.

Kody said, "You drove over Teton Pass drunk!"

"Yes. Many nights of the week I drove over it, and I was drinking."

Teton Pass crossed the state line from Wyoming into Idaho and had some of the steepest grades in the United States. It was one scary road. If you went online to the website for that pass, it suggested you find another route over those mountains. And that meant many, many miles out of your way. The website was littered with photos of upside-down trucks. In the winter the danger was multiplied by the fact that avalanche paths crossed the road. I loved to consider myself a hearty Wyoming woman, but I had checked off driving the pass in the wintertime, and in the summertime I know to be absolutely alert every moment. I didn't even glance away from the road to reach for my water bottle.

To think of Brodie driving the pass drunk was alarming — for him and for anybody else on that steep and curving two-lane. We were all appalled — Brodie himself, now stone sober, in particular.

Kody said, "That's why I'm here. One more DUI, and I'm toast. I've got four. One more, and I'm done for, off to prison, a felon, life finished. But I loved drinking beer and driving fast." He laughed, then shook his head. "But never again."

Jimmy said, "Oh, yeah, those California highways along the coast, music high, beer in my hand, stepping on the gas. I loved it too. But no more. I stopped that shit long ago. But not before I got arrested twice."

Arnie said, "That's what scares me about getting out of here on probation. I know I'll go along for a while. Hell, I've gone eight, nine months without drinking. But then along comes some girl or party and I think, 'Shoot, I could have one drink.' I get away with that and the next time I'm having a dozen drinks. Then I want to get in my car and speed down the highway... to make the night extra fun."

This talk reminded me of a conversation with an author who was in Jackson Hole to promote his book about addiction. He said, "First it's fun. Then it's fun with problems. Then it's just problems."

# [ Chapter Eighteen ]

One thing or rather another thing the inmates and I had in common was the default condition of not being in our bodies. I know this sounds like an esoteric transporting method, though clearly if the inmates could be elsewhere that would be their choice. But I mean it more in the way of not feeling our full aliveness, not being aware of how we'd numbed to our bodies. It is a common condition in our culture. We honor our intellects, our thoughts, our opinions, our gathering of knowledge, along with the degrees and titles that mark it. And it all happens above our chins. Certainly that was true for me.

Even when going outside for walks I was often in my head and had to remind myself to wake up and notice the wingbeats of a raven whooshing above me, enjoy inhaling the aroma of wet fallen aspen leaves, feel the chill wind scraping my cheeks. If I didn't alert myself to such things deliberately, I tended to rewrite paragraphs in my mind instead. A week ago, without my noticing, a branch whipped across my face while I was walking along the path. I came home and wondered what that red streak I saw in the mirror was all about. That was being out of my body.

Inmates who were addicted to anger, violence, drugs, or

alcohol were not in their bodies. They wanted the release these addictions brought them. They wanted out of their bodies; that was where the emotions, memories, and pain resided.

For me, it was a habit, something I had learned from my birth family, my culture, and used as a survival tactic. When the maestro patted my butt while I was working for him in the symphony hall, I didn't feel any dishonor, anger, or sense of being objectified. If I was lucky, another woman employee, whose butt had also been patted in the past, caught the act and we got to roll our eyes at each other. For me this hadn't required drinking or drugs to deal with; the issues hadn't marked me that severely or dented my self-esteem to that degree. But nevertheless, I was not in my body. I took refuge in not feeling. I scrambled to my head, where I could flick off the indignity.

Still, the degradation I felt at a man in power feeling he had the right to touch me that way did not dissolve over the three decades since its occurrence. The experience resided in my body, and today I am awake enough to no longer shove stuff down unexamined. And so the heap of unexamined events from my past were surfacing, layer by layer, and I needed to process them.

This processing was also part of the journaling workshop with the inmates. We uncovered layers from the past that had been shoved down into the body. I often repeated a line I wrote in my book *Writing Wild: Forming a Creative Partnership with Nature*: "What is in the light of our consciousness we can work with; what remains in the dark of our unconscious works us."

I didn't know if I was right in recommending, even urging, that the inmates look at the hard stuff. So many times I'd heard them bemoan the fact that their stories revolved around and around in their heads. They just sought relief from them without experiencing them, examining them. They felt stuck.

I suspected Lane, a man I saw every week for nearly a year, might drive himself insane with his story. His incarceration came as a result of beating up his girlfriend to the point of her needing hospitalization. Lane was bright, interesting, educated, and personable, with a good sense of humor; and he was an alcoholic in denial. I first saw him alone for a month while he was in maximum security, so we became well acquainted. He claimed he was innocent, that he'd like to beat up the man who did this to his girlfriend. I found this an odd reaction considering his alleged crime, but Lane seemed to believe that statement made him look righteously angry over his girlfriend's harm. As far as the police and local community were concerned, Lane was guilty. He spent several months in the Teton County Jail preparing for his trial and apparently rehearsing his statements and story. He admitted that he felt crazy, that the situation spun through his thoughts and prevented him from sleeping or reading or following a TV show.

By all accounts no one else could have committed this crime; the girlfriend could not have made up the story. Her experience was collaborated by cell phone photos and hospital records. The bruises on Lane's knuckles and the fingernail scratches on his cheeks when the officers tracked him down ready to board a plane didn't help his case either. Still, Lane fought it. And who could blame him? He was at risk of being determined guilty by a jury and sentenced to up to twenty years in the state prison. How do you admit to yourself what you have done while also fighting for a life free of prison bars?

Lane was thirty years old at the time of his sentence. The papers never told the whole story of his past, and Lane himself never told me, but apparently there was a prior crime of a similar nature a few years back. Lane's story was that he was wrongly accused then too. His predicament as I saw it, during the fifty meetings we had together, was that he could not tell himself the truth about the events of that night with his girlfriend. And so he circled through his story over and over like a runner training for a marathon in the small space of a jail cell. Polishing that story, practicing it, trying to inhabit it. Trying to envision how a clean-cut, honest young man of innocence might present himself to lawyers, a judge, a jury. And, each week, to me. Lane kept the wide-eyed stance of someone not knowing what people were talking about. Girl with broken jaw, loosened teeth. What? Perhaps it wasn't as difficult as I was supposing. Perhaps he was so drunk he didn't experience himself as the raging batterer he had been that night. He quite likely had disassociated from that reality.

My conundrum was how to respond with honesty to his dishonesty. All I could do was remind myself that my purpose in conducting jail workshops was to address the inner life, not the outer workings of it. I could not skirt around the necessity of honesty with oneself in discussing self-esteem, awareness, forgiveness. Or the necessity of claiming every positive and negative quality and action in one's life in order to move on.

Lane's stepfather battered him and his younger brother all through their childhood. Lane claimed to have long ago forgiven him. But Lane also claimed that alcohol was not an issue for him. As time passed I saw an entirely different picture than I once had seen while sitting across from this witty and charming guy. While meeting with Lane weekly and being on his side as a compassionate and sympathetic listener, I feared that if he didn't acknowledge his reality to himself he was going to lose his hold on sanity. What I saw eventually was a man who had already stepped over the line into mental imbalance; something about him suggested he was operating remotely. Everything continued to work for him — his charm, his intelligence, his personable manner — but he was just a well-oiled machine. Yet, even that worked for him, because the jury ended up sending him to prison for a mere three years.

Right after Lane left for his prison term, I met weekly with Brodie, who due to his being drunk and driving on the wrong side of the road, had killed a man. Brodie was sane and strong and well-balanced, and all this was entirely due, in my view, to his acknowledging the results of his actions and taking on the full horrid responsibility for them, despite being completely unaware of the event at the time because of the huge amount of alcohol he'd consumed.

It remained to be seen what would happen to either man in the future, but I'd put my money on Brodie. He was here and now, present and aware. And though he would likely serve time in prison, Brodie was going to make the best of it, sad and lonely without his family but not defeated. Mentally and emotionally stable. Most of us had been taught as children how powerful truth was, but only some of us experienced the strength it offered us in owning our actions and choices, along with the freedom to inhabit our bodies fully.

# [ Chapter Nineteen ]

You could tell Ricky was right-handed. He had a ladder of scars along his left arm, visible from just beneath his short sleeve to the top of his hand. Thin scars, as if he had used a razor blade, each an inch and a half long. He was twenty-two and came across as sweet-natured and boyish. Answers to the journaling questions revealed that he had probably been taken advantage of often. Ricky was born in Puerto Rico and had lived most of his life there. He talked about returning to help his family.

"They have no wires working," he said in his heavily accented English. Ricky and I met shortly after Hurricane Maria devastated the island. "My country has many jobs." Ricky said he knew how to repair refrigerators and cars. "Many broken cars in Puerto Rico. I can fix. Maybe sell."

Ricky likely had an issue with boundaries. He told me stories of fellow workers and so-called friends treating him poorly, and he was incarcerated for stalking a young woman. It was his second jail sentence for that crime. Both times it had been the same young woman.

Ricky didn't realize I knew that about him. He told me that his girlfriend was mad at him and that was why she had said things to put him in jail. But now she was sorry and was going with him to Puerto Rico when he was released.

This story made me question everything Ricky had told me so far about himself and his life. He looked directly at me with his warm puppy-brown eyes as he spoke, but I suspected Ricky was incapable of recognizing reality. The other men stayed silent but exchanged slight smiles.

I didn't need to catch anyone in a lie, but neither did it feel right to nod and smile at obvious falsehoods. It wasn't good for any of us to get away with that. Successful repetitions of false stories strengthened them, and soon the manufactured story held more vitality than the actual event. Many people felt innocent as long as others saw them that way. Like the riddle of whether a tree falling in the forest makes a sound if nobody was there to hear it, for some of us reality doesn't exist unless someone else witnesses it. I came across this often. Inmates wanted to tell me their versions of why they were wrongly arrested. Sometimes I knew the truth of their guilt, and I watched how their earnest eyes sought belief in my face. I won't play, but neither do I challenge them.

Things got out of hand during this workshop. All the men were new inmates. After Ricky told his outlandish story about his so-called girlfriend, Jed tried to convince me he didn't rob his employer's storeroom, despite film proving he did; Davy didn't really do a hit-and-run, he had meant to report the accident pretty soon, and besides, the guy got up and walked away; and Sam was only napping with that whiskey bottle under his arm at 3:00 a.m. in the town square. I held up a hand — a pressing of the pause button. And I said, "The journaling workshop is all about the inner life, not the outer life and how that didn't turn out well for you."

Chuck: "That's because that shit cop..."

Halt with the hand again.

"So we talk about personal power, self-compassion, and understanding ourselves." I don't mention the hard stuff like anger and forgiveness yet. "Already I know you are survivors. Whatever brought you to this moment and this place was all about you just trying to make it in a world that seems to do its best to push you off course." All five guys in the circle resonated to my recognition of life as a bitch.

I said, "I admire survivors."

I fingered through my stack of index cards that for most people held recipes but held favorite quotes for me. "This is a quote from Rumi: 'The wound is the place where the light enters you.'" I looked at each of them. "Wherever we hurt, that's the place we've become available to our own wisdom. Each of you is meant to contribute something to life. This is a good time to gather some clues about what that might be."

Though I didn't say so, I trusted life, and if that meant an arrest, perhaps that was the very thing needed in each case. My message of using the time of incarceration to go inward for renewal, for inquiry, for empowering oneself was worth repeating.

Typically, the inmates promoted their case as a guilt-free arrest only during the first week of incarceration. I translated this urge as a desire for me to see them as who they were outside their current circumstances. And since that was the entire basis of my meeting them on Tuesday nights, I relayed that perspective rather quickly. Often the other inmates would have already laid that out for the new guys. That may even be the reason they attended the workshop. Perhaps they had heard that our talk had nothing to do with their arrest or their crime or their past court records. I saw the men at their rawest more often than not. They came to the workshop with souls naked, wanting to understand themselves, feel decent about their past lives, hopeful about their future lives.

At that point the jail held a small population of inmates, most of them recently arrested. They didn't yet know that they could trust me to see them as they truly were, hence the stories of innocence, the blaming of others. They wanted to begin our relationship on equal footing and knew no other way. They had been at war — with the cops, the community, the economy, and often their own bodies — through addiction.

We all wanted peace…unless disruption served us better, distracting us, as it can, from our impotence or misery.

# [ Chapter Twenty ]

Pain and addiction go together like watermelon and seeds. Pain begets addiction, and addiction seeds further pain. When life is too agonizing to endure, numbing beckons, and though the subject of addiction contains layers and facets and unfathomed mysteries, it was safe to surmise that not one of the thousands of inmates I'd met with was an addict for the fun of it. And nearly every inmate I'd encountered over the years of volunteering at my county jail was arrested in part as a result of his addiction. Suffering, a longing to escape reality, a desire to buffer one's life — the reasons stretched on, yet all added up to one thing: shutting down full awareness.

Joseph Campbell wrote, "People say what we're all seeking is a meaning for life. I don't think that's what we're really seeking. I think what we're seeking is an experience of being alive." It may be called a form of insanity not to want the experience of being alive. And yet there are millions of us who find ways to avoid feeling our full measure of aliveness through drugs and alcohol.

This is what is requested of addicts and alcoholics: that they alter past routines and drop old friends, build new life structures and create new relationships. Sobriety demands structuring entire new identities. Lewis Hyde, in an essay about the author and alcoholic John Berryman, wrote that if Berryman had stopped drinking and not thrown himself off a bridge to his death, "he would have had to leave his friends who had helped him live off his pain for twenty years." I discovered this quote in the book *The Recovering: Intoxication and its Aftermath* by Leslie Jamison. And it reminded me of how often I heard from the inmates that this demand to change their friends was the most difficult thing and often the one thing they could not do. They didn't know themselves in any other way than stopping at the bar after work for a drink with their friends, staying for another, missing dinner, drinking until late, hoping to drive home without incident, stumbling into bed. Work, drink, bed. Repeat.

For a person to leave their life of addiction and the companions from that life, who often supported and encouraged it, they need to possess a strong center of personal power. There has to be firm grounding at their core and an awareness of strength beyond their life situation. To step into the unknown, even when convinced it's the life-saving route, was a lonely and fearful decision to make.

I had been daring myself for the past few years to bring more spirituality to the journaling workshops in order to address this very issue. I wanted to discuss the spiritual in a universal form that essentially spoke of Life, capital *L*, to the inmates who had survived up to this point by numbing themselves to their lives. How could a person be required to alter their outward behavior without reawakening or creating a deep relationship with their inward self? I had been reluctant to enter this most intimate and private place. I didn't feel qualified. I was scared, really.

Though, if I were bold enough, this is what I'd like to say:

"There are many similarities between your experience as an inmate in jail and a monk's in a monastery. You have work to do here. Inner work. Begin it. Conduct inquiry into your sense of self, asking why, how, when, who; offer your mind the ideas of others through reading; examine yourself by journaling your memories, dreams, intentions, strengths, and weaknesses. Lay it all open. Claim it. Face it. Let it out, so the process of letting it go can begin. And please, befriend yourself throughout with kindness and understanding."

I wanted to urge them to live in the present moment as often as possible, saying, "Halt those old stories revolving through the mind about who hurt you and who you hurt."

If I could, I would like to make the inmates comfortable with an inner stillness, where joy had a chance to emerge within the cement walls of their jail cells. I wanted to tell them, "Your real life lies beneath your life situation." Though I've never used the word, it was the soul within each inmate that I spoke to, that core spiritual self. Rumi said that well: "Out beyond ideas of wrongdoing and rightdoing/there is a field, I'll meet you there." That was where our workshops took place.

But who was I to tell these men there was something more than old hurts from the past or fears for the future? I was on the wrong side of six locked doors to have the right to convince them that joy and goodness were available to them. They were beaten bloody by fathers, abandoned by their mothers. Their foster parents told them they were not worth the sparse food they were reluctantly fed; they attended school where the kids jeered at their handed-down clothing and crude haircuts. Wherever they looked there was meanness, lack, fear. And I should be presumptuous enough to tell them that life was more than what they had tried to drink and drug their way out of?

I was not that bold. Not yet. But I yearned to tell them just that. And I wanted to convince them that they must provide for themselves all that had been withheld from them in the way of love, compassion, understanding, and support. And that they must learn to do this without any role models to show them how.

I wanted to say this to the men: "Inside, you are someone who yearns for things perhaps unseen and never experienced: family love, trusted friends, good work, comfort, home, purpose. You deserve to have all this. Trust that imagined life coming from within; follow those longings."

I wanted to say: "You are in the darkness of life. All beginnings start there. They start in the dark and reach for imagined light. You are a seed in the dark earth, and somewhere deep within the hull of you, you sense warmth and light and fulfillment. Trust that. Push through the dark earth, and one day there will be sunshine and you will feel yourself beginning to swell and stretch. Even now you are becoming. It all begins here, in this jail, in this darkness."

I wanted to offer the inmates these words from author and activist Christine Caine: "Sometimes when you're in a dark place you think you've been buried, but really you've been planted."

# [ Chapter Twenty-One ]

When meeting with the inmates I rarely considered whether they were guilty of the crimes for which they'd been arrested. I expressed interest in their court appearances and lawyer meetings as a way of keeping track of what mattered to them, but I made sure we spent most of our time together exploring the inner life. Or as I told the guys often: there is your life situation, and then there is your life. I had learned over the years that this helped them to separate behavior they often regretted from the human beings they otherwise were. So after catching up with what had happened for each of them legally, we moved into the journaling questions for the evening.

Carl, a man in his midthirties, had been coming to the workshop for nearly a year, never missing the weekly session. His steady presence gave a sense of continuity to the workshop, which deepened our group's discussions week after week. He and I became familiar with each other's stories. I enjoyed his brightness and quick humor, and we often found we liked the same authors. Most of all I enjoyed how Carl seemed to become more and more interested in discovering what mattered in life. He was actively seeking a purpose and had discovered that it was helping his fellow inmates whenever he could. He was teaching two Spanish-speaking men English and helping another inmate learn to read. If there was such a thing as a teacher's pet in the workshop, I guess Carl was mine that year. At the time he was the only inmate I had spent a few dozen consecutive hours with.

Incriminating news stories about his alleged crime hit the papers every time Carl went to court during the months leading up to his jury trial, and each time he was unfailingly adamant with the judge about his innocence. In our workshop Carl skirted the issue of his innocence or guilt, and I was thankful that he kept that out of our meetings. However, he reported to us his assurance that the trial would go well for him. His family had hired a detective who had discovered new evidence, and expert witnesses were lined up to testify at his trial. It sounded as though his defense was strongly supported. His parents were laying out a lot of money and traveled from New York to attend all his hearings and to visit, bringing along his sister and two brothers.

His alleged crime: beating up his live-in boyfriend to the point of hospitalization. There were Carl's bloody clothes, splatters in their shared condo, and the hospital documentation to bolster the boyfriend's claim that Carl had inflicted the injuries that resulted in a wired jaw and skull fractures, along with other injuries only alluded to in the news stories. However, Carl claimed to the court that a fall down the icy outdoor staircase of their condo building was behind it all.

Personally, I believed that Carl was tending to his inner life, growing in awareness, working at forgiveness — for himself and others — and that whatever he said in the courtroom was strictly for the sake of survival, to keep himself out of prison and perhaps to stay in the good graces of his family members.

Though I have met a man who tried to convince me he was arrested and jailed in maximum security for failing to use his left-hand turn signal, after the first week or so of incarceration most of the inmates were forthcoming about their crimes, which anchored our workshop in meaningful exchanges. As was typical with me, the question of Carl's innocence or guilt didn't interest me as much as the man himself and the growth I enjoyed witnessing.

At least that was how I saw myself, until one night toward the end of Carl's incarceration in the Teton County Jail. I asked this question in our journaling group: "When did you know you could survive betrayal, disappointment, or other emotional pain that had entered your life?"

From the other six inmates I heard stories of child abuse, a suicidal parent, an unfaithful wife, the death of someone beloved. From Carl I heard, "March fourteen, the night my boyfriend betrayed me to the police."

No neon lights blinked around those words. No quiz-show buzzer rasped out that it was the wrong answer. And yet. And yet, I couldn't lift my eyes to look at him. A recognition rose through my body that Carl was a flat-out liar... and had been suckered into believing his own false claims. I didn't feel shocked as much as disgusted. During his year of attending the workshop Carl had expressed no concern for his boyfriend's suffering, regardless of how he had acquired his injuries, and now Carl was acting as if he were the injured victim.

Something so false rang from those words that I didn't want to let anyone see my face. All along I had assumed that Carl, innocent or guilty, was dealing with his inner life while fighting however he needed to for his outer life. Now I felt fearful for Carl because he had acted innocent for so long in so many different settings to so many different people that I sensed he was a smiling O.J. Simpson who had no connection whatsoever to his inner reality.

The money his parents invested in his case worked in Carl's favor in the courtroom. That was, it worked somewhat in his favor, though not to the degree Carl hoped. The hired detective was able to stir up enough doubt to nudge the court into offering Carl a plea deal but likely not enough to get an innocent verdict from a trial jury.

I thought back to the year of intimate talk with Carl, listening to him tell of his past abuse from his grandfather, cheerleading on his behalf when he sank into depression, being happy for him when something legal went his way and then that moment of chill when I realized that he had fooled not just me but, more direly, himself. That year of personal growth I shared with Carl all along had been rooted in a dark and twisted falseness. Throughout the rest of his life he would need to maintain and feed this falseness to the people who mattered most to him: his parents, his sister, and his two brothers. And over the next weeks while the legal process snailed its way to sentencing, Carl needed to uphold this falseness with the detention officers, his fellow cellmates, his lawyer, the judge, and yes, me.

Did anyone ever recover from the depths of such self-deception? And what, I wondered, did Carl get out of meeting with me week after week, portraying himself as a man who was engaged in inquiry, seeking personal truth?

When it was time for Carl to accept or reject the offer of the court, I felt validated in my deep suspicion of his guilt.

Because Carl pleaded nolo contendere, no contest.

That was a plea a guilty person generally agreed to when it offered the best outcome they could hope for. The plea limited his prison time from likely multiple decades to at most one decade and probably less. In the end he was sentenced to eight years in the Wyoming penitentiary, and I never encountered him again.

The situation with Carl required that I go with the flow and be at ease with the circumstances of the moment and, though I was thrown off center for less than a minute, I had missed that mark.

Wisdom teachers from many traditions suggest that we become comfortable with not-knowing, because this is, of course, the rude reality. We don't know. Anything. Ever. We just love thinking we do. Wisdom teachers suggest we remain poised firmly in the present. A perspective that held no hopes or fears. Yet I couldn't seem to drive two miles to the grocery store without hoping I'd make all the green lights or fearing that the store had run out of hazelnut chocolate bars. The state of not-knowing was uncomfortable to me. I set up my life so that I knew there was bakery bread for my toast in the morning, along with a full canister of finely ground French roast. And when the TV guide claimed a *Downton Abbey* rerun would be aired at eight that evening, I was damned upset when it didn't.

But my job in the jail, and in life, was to become comfortable with not-knowing. It wasn't enough for me to be unbiased about an inmate's innocence or guilt; I needed to be just as dispassionate about why an inmate attended the workshop, even if it was to find a reflection of innocence in my eyes when they were guilty as hell.

It was really none of my business.

Carl reminded me of that.

# [ Chapter Twenty-Two ]

When I read the news stories about the arrests of men who were accused of beating up their girlfriends, charged by their wives of strangulation attempts, or found negligent or abusive to children, I felt angry. Furious, in fact.

Yet when the Tuesday-night journaling workshop rolled around, somehow that fury dissolved instantly in the presence of the man himself. Suddenly I was aware that we were all beings just trying to make it. During our talk I would learn, once again, that everything was interconnected, that this violent crime did not stand alone but was related to so much else, beginning with the man's experience of violence in his childhood.

At the moment of meeting face-to-face, none of that was conscious. What I was aware of was that before me was a human and that I was a human too. Something sacred arose with that awareness. The space between us felt clean, not laden with his actions or my beliefs. He and I were just *there*.

Some other part of me greeted some other part of the inmate. It was — whatever "it" was — so fully formed as to be incontestable. This space in which we met could not be tampered with; it was inviolable, and in the face of it, my anger didn't even make an appearance.

I didn't understand it.

I could explain my reaction away mentally when I tried: It was not my job to make anyone accountable; there were agencies and courtrooms for that. But this fact didn't really tell me anything, even though I usually felt more confident of my inner responses when I could find logic or reasoning to support my position.

The space between the accused inmate and me pulsed with a soft glow that was timeless and faceless and, really, pointless. There was no goal, no point to our meeting. He was there; I was there. We were two people being there together — him sitting on a gray plastic chair locked in the room on his side of the metal grate, me sitting in that ratty orange upholstered chair locked in my room on my side of the grate. Yet I never again viewed the man the way I did when reading about his crime in the newspaper.

The experience felt sacred. It lifted me. And that fact might be my entrance into solving this puzzle. I was not meeting with an accused criminal, I was meeting with — and this was what stopped me, for I had no language for what I was meeting, unless it was myself in another disguise. I experienced an alive energetic presence in human form. And that was sacred. And so if I were to put words to what happened, I would say that my sacred energy met another's.

This never failed to hold up. I could learn further brutal details of a man's alleged crime, and still it was me, the essence of my aliveness, meeting with him, the essence of his aliveness.

Maybe I did understand it. Maybe it was as simple as that.

Recently this experience was put to a serious test.

A story in the local newspaper about a man accused of horrific violence toward his girlfriend had drilled deeply into my mind. He was arrested, went to court, allowed out on bail, and fled the state with a new girlfriend. I shuddered in revulsion every time the images of his abusive acts toward his former girlfriend came to mind. And I feared for his new girlfriend. Did she know who she had *really* left town with? Was she too experiencing violence from this man? A month passed, and another news story reported that the man I'll call Martin had been found and arrested by officers from a West Coast state. Next he would be extradited back to Wyoming. Then one day, when I checked the Teton County online site listing inmates in custody, I spotted Martin's photo. He was in maximum security.

I had been visiting Abel, a young well-read Mexican man with whom I had been enjoying book discussions, in max. I liked how Abel read carefully, taking in ideas and testing them against his own perspectives. So Tuesday night when Officer Lana listed the different groups I'd be meeting with — two women, three inmate workers, a group of C cell inmates, and one man from max — I let out my breath. One man from max, not two. I would be seeing Abel. Only.

For days, even weeks, after reading a description of Martin's extremely abusive acts against his girlfriend, I would have to pause in whatever I was doing and concentrate on my breathing in order to move forward. Considering that, I wondered at how smoothly I accepted being face-to-face with this very man when it was Martin, not Abel, who came down from max. It was what I took on as a volunteer, of course, and I was not alone in dealing with such a challenge. Yet once home I questioned myself over how easy it was for me to address him in person. I did not cringe from him, not in the slightest. It was as if I were a different being from the one who read the newspaper during my lunch break in my cabin. I was a clean slate sitting with him. I did not have to shove aside a shade of discomfort or judgment or abhorrence, all of which I had felt repeatedly at the mere thought of this man's actions before that night.

But that was it: there were his actions and then there was him as a human being. While reading the news story, I was viewing him through the labels given him, his behavior, and his life situation, not him as an alive being. Although reading about him had triggered a sense of fear as a woman, I felt none of that as we stood facing each other. I did not even feel surprised that it was this man, Martin, instead of my old familiar inmate and fellow literary reader, Abel.

After a moment we sat and introduced ourselves through the metal grate. Within our allotted thirty minutes, our relationship deepened into an intimacy that felt like it dissolved the grate. Martin had a nice smile, clear eyes. He was present with me, and honest to the degree we needed in order to talk about the inner life.

"I don't think I really know myself," Martin said, "now that I think of it." He dipped his head, then lifted it again to look at me. "That's it, isn't it? I never thought of it."

"That's what this time is all about. If life was intent on taking good care of you, maybe this is exactly the place for you to do your most important work. You think?"

"Yeah, could be."

"Going inward is where all the freedom lies. Same for me on this side of the grate. Would you say addiction of any kind is part of your reason for being jailed?"

"Yeah, for sure. My life is successful — anything I try to do, I succeed at doing — but I fail big-time when I drink. All my trouble has come from drinking." He looked down toward the ledge set against the grate where he rested his arms. My arms rested on my side of the ledge.

I said, "What I have learned is that beneath the addiction is pain."

Martin's head snapped up.

"Sound right?" I asked.

"Oh yeah, I've been shoving stuff down for years. I don't know what else to do with it."

"Look at it. Claim it. Do it in small steps, don't overwhelm yourself. You're in solitary confinement with little to distract you. So write a bit about your life, dredge up some sore memories, then make yourself exercise. Run in place, whatever you can do in your small space. Read something enjoyable. Look at your life a bit more. And here's the big piece: write a list of your strengths, your good qualities.

I tell him the Masai story. I embellish it by adding that I traveled to Africa and visited a Masai village — all true. Though as I've mentioned before, the story itself may not be so true. I liked telling it anyway.

"And each person in the village told this man every good thing they could remember about him from the day he was born. Because... they believed he had just forgotten." And I also added that our culture didn't handle behavior against the community that way; rather, we tended to blame, to use guilt and shame, and therefore we had to remind ourselves of every good thing about us.

Martin listened carefully. He responded appropriately, and he said three times, "I'm so glad I came down to see you. I didn't know what I was coming to." I could have been spooning hearty soup to a starving man.

Perhaps that's a better explanation of how it went that

night. Presented with a starving man, every single one of us would have spooned nourishing soup into the empty bowl he held. Not one of us would have wondered if he were worthy of the soup or if we should have withheld the meatier ingredients or feared that something from his past might affect us. Maybe I had taken in what I so often tell the men: there is your life situation, and there is your Life, that astonishing light within that Hafiz speaks of. Who could resist providing fuel to build up that light enough for its owner to believe in its existence?

And so I kept going. I gave him my favorite quotes, which I had memorized. I told him about the hero's journey, the belly of the whale, about personal power. I told him about listing three people he admired and all their qualities, so I could disclose to a man in need the great good news that these qualities also belonged to him.

Later I realized this was a gift my jail workshops had given me: an unshakable inner calm, rooted in acceptance of whatever the moment brought. This wasn't a detachment from the situation, a shield put in place to give me time to adjust; it was an always open door, a sense of availability. I felt present and comfortable and welcoming.

This feeling didn't necessarily carry over into my daily life. All I needed to do was open the lid of the washing machine I shared with my former husband, now housemate, and discover his wet Levi's coiled at the bottom, smelling like they'd been there for three days, while my arms were piled with my own laundry ready to load, and I'd let loose expletives, loud and clear.

Transformation took place in jail cells. It was, in fact, intended to. No candles or meditation zafus were allowed. No Celtic bells, Tibetan singing bowls, or rosary beads. But as sure as a monastery cell, the Teton County Jail cell is a sacred space. Contemplation and prayer, devotional reading and self-examination, centering and clarifying occurred there. When I asked the inmates to list in their journals their strengths and weaknesses, we were engaging in the process of inquiry, a divine searching inward. We were finding ourselves.

When Bill Moyer asked Joseph Campbell during a PBS interview years ago what it meant to have a sacred space, Campbell said, "This is . . . a place where you can simply experience and bring forth what you are and what you might be. This is a place of creative incubation."

Yet most people, when considering the inmates, were left solely with their reactions to the newspaper stories. And that included the many people who now had say over the inmates' incarceration, legal defense, and courtroom decisions. There was little to no discussion in the community about supporting the incarcerated men and women in their search for change and improvement — by offering them larger libraries, e-readers so they could do research, rehabilitation funds, educational opportunities, and possibly the most valuable offering, more interaction with the community itself. Classes, discussion groups, meditation, and yoga guidance.

The inmates had demonstrated over and over to me their desire to improve their lives, but when there was no way to do that, they lost momentum. Apathy set in. They resorted to watching more TV and sleeping during the day.

The detention center was the most ignored institution in the county.

• • • •

As it turned out, it was just as well that I loaded Martin up with everything I could possibly feed him in thirty minutes.

He seemed to genuinely take it in, feel nourished, and curious about learning more about himself. But I never saw him again.

He was incarcerated for five months following our meeting before the court sent him to prison. But he chose to never again meet with me or, once allowed into the general population, to attend our group workshops. In the seven years I had volunteered to conduct weekly journaling workshops that had never happened before.

# [ Chapter Twenty-Three ]

Last night a new guy, Vance, came down to the workshop and by way of introduction said he had been arrested for possession. Sandy, the inmate sitting next to him, pointed to himself and said, "Possession *and* delivery." Next they were checking in with each other: "What's your drug of choice?" I watched as a feeling of brotherhood rose between them. They had things in common: drug use, incarceration, and all that led from one to the other. An eagerness to exchange stories lit up their faces.

Joseph Campbell has discussed in interviews and talks how women's menstruation serves as a shared sisterly milestone of growth. It ushers a girl into womanhood, unifies a sense of the feminine, and opens life to the possibility of motherhood, or service to the community, something beyond herself, something larger and meaningful. Many aboriginal cultures create events to help lead boys into manhood. Rituals and body markings, and even pain are used, the way pain is part of women's experience of giving birth. Such events encourage bonding and allow a man to experience personal growth while also witnessing this growth reflected by his companions. Was the glow on the faces of Vance and Sandy tribal recognition?

There was camaraderie there; they could barely stop

exchanging stories so our workshop could resume. Sandy said, "I wish you were in my cell block; we've got a lot to talk about." That this longing to be part of something larger than oneself — a community, a movement, a shared experience — could be so fierce that a person would seek it through self-destructive behavior wrenched my heart. Yet this idea kept appearing during our workshops.

When Terrance talked about not being willing to give up going to bars, even though he was currently jailed for the third time for public inebriation, I felt like he was saying, "Those are my people. I have to be with them, no matter what."

Two years after this meeting Sandy was killed in a car accident while under the influence of several drugs, according to news reports. He and I shared a pleasant history over the years of meeting during his three incarcerations. I enjoyed his caring nature and ability to be honest about himself. My sorrow over Sandy's death is stirred each time an inmate is incarcerated repeatedly for his addiction. And I'm reminded of the fierce struggle and the dire risks involved.

One night we finished our journaling and workshop discussion early and began to talk casually. In no time the conversation among the men drifted into closing time at the bar. Saying goodbye, finding ways to extend the gathering. Sometimes that meant destroying property as a group, starting fights, racing in cars, finding drug dealers since there were no closing hours for that business. Again I felt that what they were really discussing was loneliness, a desire to continue the tribal oneness that drinking opened for them. Gangs were based on this yearning to bond, and individuals put their lives in danger to maintain their acceptance within the group. The hazing rituals of fraternities, same deal.

Campbell referred to caves as sacred spaces when he discussed the symbolic paintings found in them as far back as thirty thousand years ago. He said, "Sacred space, then, is any area, such as the caves, in which everything is done to transform the environment into a metaphor." Bars had become the holy places of shared experience for some. To get high, to get drunk, to have hangovers were almost rituals and were condoned by the surroundings. In one local bar even the clock encouraged overuse, boasting a beer ad that said in orange neon, "Stagger on up for another." And now I saw that the men in jail were in another tribal situation, bonded by the past and their resistance to the present.

The following Tuesday night we talked about this idea of sacred space. I referred to incarceration as belly of the whale time, as cave time. A sacred time. Brodie said, "That's why I'm drawing a lot. It makes me feel quiet, like I'm in church."

I said, "Yes, like a spiritual retreat, like living in a monastery." I glanced around, checking for eye rolls, but instead I spotted agreement with head nods from the others besides Brodie — Lonnie, AJ, Dan.

Lonnie said, "I know I've changed over the past eight months I've been here. I feel more definite as a person. Like, I know me better. I'm stronger. I can tell."

I welcomed this realization from Lonnie. He was a naturally kind man but a follower. He never missed a workshop in all his months of incarceration and often brought new inmates along with him. He was thirty-eight years old. His mother sounded rather small-minded and a bit cruel, and his girlfriend, with whom he had a toddler son, sounded like a duplicate of her. I suspected people often took advantage of Lonnie and that he just as often found excuses for them and himself. My hope for him was just what he expressed: a more defined and positive self-image. Basically it seemed he had been jailed because he was too nice: he didn't sell drugs, he gave them away.

Perhaps saying that Lonnie is too nice is another way of saying he lacked confidence in himself and wasn't convinced of his own worthiness. And this resulted in weak boundaries.

As I've mentioned, this is something I have lived with myself — trouble saying no, even to my dogs. Just the other day I let Zoe pull her leash, with me attached, across the pathway into the oncoming lane near a curve because she smelled something interesting. I caught myself thinking, I hope no fast bikes whip around that curve and we cause a wreck. I mentally slapped myself and got both of us back into our own lane. But I marked the occasion as a frayed rope in my boundary system.

In the workshop AJ held up his journal and fanned the pages for me to see where he'd densely written his thoughts. "Three months of taking notes about what I'm reading and thinking. Sometimes I write down quotes that I come across. I see more clearly now how I was living my life. Heck, I'd have two beers before going to work in the morning, and that was just the start of my drinking day. I know I don't want to live like that anymore. Now I've got interesting things to think about. I didn't used to do anything but drink and work before."

This was quite an admission from AJ. When he first joined the workshop he carefully explained to me and the group that he was no longer going to take drugs. "Beer," he had said, "that's not an issue for me. I can have beer, but no more cocaine." He'd come a long way in being truthful with himself.

Dan said, "I've been raising my two kids alone back home in Georgia. I had to stop doing my usual work so I could be available to run the kids to sports practice and a bunch of stuff. They've graduated now, and I got time. I should start giving some to myself. I never had a minute before, not for years. I started drinking and got into trouble. But now I'm reading and reading and reading. I feel like — yeah, kind of like a monk in a monastery — like I can just be thinking about my life. I might be here for just a month more, and I hope that's enough time."

What I wanted to promote to the guys — a kind of inner stillness, a befriending of themselves — sometimes took hold in wonderfully satisfying sessions, as it had this night.

# [ Chapter Twenty-Four ]

One theme I kept coming back to with the men was that often we try to make others feel the way we are feeling. It was a perspective I passed on to the inmates during our workshop one night when they complained about a particular officer.

"Nevel treats us like garbage. He even calls us that."

"Yeah, every chance he gets, Officer Nevel puts us down."

"And tries to make everything hard. Like, he makes a huge bunch of noise when he does bed checks every hour during the night to deliberately disturb us, and he walks around the exercise machines sneering at us."

I said, "Aww, Officer Nevel is miserable. He feels like crap." I noted the surprise on the guys' faces but ignored it. "He feels he has no real power, and so far that's been his experience: that nothing goes his way. He may be suffering from depression; he certainly has low self-esteem. And he is not nice to himself at all. Probably looks in the mirror every morning when he shaves and insults himself about his looks, his intelligence, and his chances of getting anything he dreams about. Likely he feels that nothing is fair in the world and that he might as well forget about expecting anything good to happen to him." I went on like that for a bit, until the surprise was wiped off the guys' faces and they got that this guy who seemed to have the upper hand was in reality someone to be pitied. That, in fact, happy, contented people who felt good about themselves and their place in life did not have an interest in making anyone else feel bad.

But, man, was it hard to feel sympathy for this guy. Officer Nevel pulled that kind of crap on me too, and I almost lost it every time. When he was the officer assigned to greeting me in the lobby, he started right off with a smirky smile.

"We're too busy to take you upstairs to the tower. You can meet the inmates in CV 2."

I knew that would be the case as soon as he appeared. But I didn't object, since doing so had proven to be useless. This officer had been known to squeeze five men into the tiny grated room designed for one.

I passed Officer Nevel the number of journals needed for newcomers and gave him two pencils for each man.

"They don't need two. Just one," Nevel said.

"When the lead breaks on one pencil it ends our workshop for that man."

"One pencil. That's the law. It's a safety issue." Slight smile.

There was no law, no safety issue. These were three-inch-long golf pencils, and I'd been passing out two to each man every week for several years before Nevel showed up. But I said none of that. I nodded and moved on. Let him swing his meager control around if he needed to. But I had to take a moment to calm the fury that rose in my chest, riding on the strong yearning to take this bully down a few notches. Mainly I had to fight the urge to express rage or dismissal in my eyes. I wanted so much to return his smirk and glare at him. But that was not going to do me or the inmates any good.

I sympathized with the guys' complaints and confessed my own urges to do as my mother used to say: break his arm off and hit him over the head with it. But what was needed here most was to listen to the men. AJ put it well: "Just because we are in jail people shouldn't think of us as lesser human beings. We are just as valuable humans as they are. We made mistakes, we are addicts, we committed acts against the laws, and we are in here paying a price for that. We are no less important than others. Yet people discount us because we're in jail. We're inmates. Like that's some creation other than a human and not as good."

This was not the time for it, but I made a note to plan a journaling session in the near future about not taking things personally. I had done that exercise before and found it difficult for people to accept. It felt *so* personal when someone looked us straight in the eye, used our name, and insulted us.

When my former husband said he'd rather own a motorcycle than sell it to fund hearing aids that would allow us to talk to each other, I took that personally. When Mike's foster mother told him he was a pile of shit and smelled like it and always would, he took it personally, even twenty years later sitting in jail. When Officer Nevel called Ray by name, sneered into his face, and told him to forget about putting his boots on in preparation for his release because a new warrant "just now" came in, Ray took it personally.

And yet in each case the words and intention to hurt said more about the speaker than it ever did about the person to whom the words and ugly feelings were directed. But try to convince us of that when we are bleeding inside.

Bobby was seething in anger. He had served in Afghanistan and came home to people who were getting mad when someone cut them off on the highway or didn't make their latte with enough foam. He took that personally.

"I fight a war for my country and come home to discover they are a bunch of whiny wimps that don't even appreciate the sun shining on them. I got injured. My back hurts, my mind is full of screams and blood and monstrous images. Nobody said thanks. They said they don't got a job for me, that I can't afford to rent a bedroom in a crummy house, that I already spent enough free nights in the mission, that I can't even get drunk enough to kill myself without being thrown in jail."

When I talked about not taking anything personally to Bobby, he shook his head throughout. "It is personal. It is. My family won't even help me out. Said I shouldn't be in jail, that I was messed up and that they didn't want to have anything to do with me. *Me.* That's personal."

I said, "I get you. I understand. Just put that perspective on a shelf in your mind. Take it out and see what you think about it once in a while." Nothing more needed.

The inmates tested me and my philosophy, and I grew because of it. It was hard to explain to myself what happened in our journaling sessions. It felt like one big soup of exchange to me. And I have reason to believe it felt that way to the inmates as well. I don't think they saw me as who I was outside the jail, except perhaps the first time we met. After that, I don't think they viewed me according to my work or my economic status or my role in the community. That hour for me and for the inmates loomed apart from ordinary life. We met in an almost disembodied way, as transparent beings of emotion attached to memories, dreams, fears, hopes. I believed that at least for that hour of our workshop we took nothing personally, no matter who had said it.

# [ Chapter Twenty-Five ]

I told my writing students it was vital to include sensory material in our fiction and nonfiction. Our five senses — sight, sound, smell, taste, and touch — were our powerlines to the world around us. My book *Writing Wild* revolved around this idea. Our senses were our library, our way of connecting with the world, our palette for describing experiences to ourselves and others, and our pathway to a greater sense of aliveness. But when you were incarcerated in a county jail cell, your surroundings abruptly become colorless and without texture; the food tasteless; the smells — if lucky — antiseptic; and the sounds abrasive, raucous, disruptive, and continuous. To be present in our body, to enjoy our senses, and to track our emotional sensations as they move through us is to experience aliveness. And yet there was little to invite the inmates to awaken to their aliveness during incarceration.

Most inmates have addiction issues that played a part in their crime and arrest, and yet even in a situation of enforced sobriety, there was nothing to encourage them to stay alert rather than to numb out. Instead, the surroundings encouraged a form of numbness other than alcohol or drugs, such as daytime sleeping and hours and hours of TV watching.

The inmates are surrounded by beige-painted cement walls, concrete floors, metal furnishings, stagnant air, artificial light. No windows, no fresh breezes, no sunlight.

Once an inmate, celled alone for months, told me he was allowed outside for a bit before we met, and a chickadee had landed on top of the cement wall enclosure. His eyes glistened as he told me how beautiful the bird was, how special it was that the bird had happened to fly to his space just as he was allowed outside. "I felt a part of the world again," he said.

So as I talked in the workshop about how the thing we all wanted most in the world, no matter where we were or who we were, was aliveness, I felt as if I was dangling something that deliberately had been put out of reach for the inmates. And yet I believed the most powerful weapon they were ever going to have in their arsenal for saving themselves from addiction and crime, and the shame and guilt and fear that came with those conditions, was reaching for aliveness. Again, as Joseph Campbell wrote, "People say we all want to know the meaning of life. I don't believe that's what we want. What we want is the experience of feeling alive."

I had never been an inmate or, before conducting the workshops, in contact with anyone who had been an inmate, so I can only describe what being in the detention center one or two hours a week felt like. There was a dearth of sensory input. The only color I saw, aside from beige, was that of the inmates' two-piece outfits. Red-and-white striped for inmate workers, bile-yellow for those in maximum security, gray striped for the general population. For texture there are the painted-over bumps of the cement-block walls, the gray plastic lawn chairs, the metal tables secured to the floor of each cell block, with attached stools.

On a rare visit, I was taken into a typical cell block where an inmate was detained alone. Due to his alleged crime of child sexual abuse he was held in an area separated from the general population until his court appearance. There he and I held a journaling session. I sat on the small metal stool attached to the metal table and slipped right off. In fact, I slipped off once more before my bottom managed to balance itself on the rounded stool top. This made me laugh, but the woman officer escorting me just stared at me flat-eyed. Once I realized she was trying to discern my sobriety, it made my third attempt to stay on the tiny smooth stool top tense with an urgency to succeed. But to sit on that metal knob for half an hour made me long for a cushion. The inmates have no other place to sit in order to write, watch TV, or talk together.

The noise in the jail was deafening at times. Not to mention upsetting, as there were inmates, coming down off drugs or alcohol, who were yelling and banging. Sometimes mental patients were incarcerated for weeks, awaiting a bed in another institution. Metal doors slammed continuously.

In an intimate discussion during one workshop, I was let in on how very miserable it could be to share space with strangers. "I try to convince the new guys that come in to please not have bowel movements just prior to mealtime," Arnold said. "It's just minimal decency, but I'm not always successful in getting that across. This place can be disgusting in ways outsiders cannot imagine."

# [ Chapter Twenty-Six ]

This morning I was sitting beside Cache Creek, facing Snow King Mountain. I'd brought my notebook and breakfast, an everything bagel with Mexican cream cheese and a Wild Tribe, that treat of slushy espresso, cream, and, chocolate.

The sky was a cloudless lake of blue with three raptors floating the currents. Above the creek mayflies sparked sunshine as they lifted and dipped near the water's surface, making any trout below wiggle with anticipation. I was breakfasting just a few blocks from the county jail, beneath the same blue sky, and if the inmates were allowed any views out the windows, they too could count the many shades of green along the slope of Snow King. The ski runs showed brilliant new green growth, lined by black-green pines; lower on the slope lime-green aspen leaves spun on their stems, tossing glitter into the sky.

Just a couple of weeks ago these slopes looked like the rumps of Appaloosa ponies with their spotty snow fields dotting brown grass. The trees were bony skeletons against the pale sky. And snow flurries whipped through within minutes, leaving damp, fragrant trails of freshness in the air. Now the last ice shelves along Flat Creek had toppled into the warmer water and melted. Tall grasses held fawns, and pebbles held killdeer eggs, speckled like the rocks themselves.

Once in a while an inmate would speak with wonder about a two-inch crack in the permanent window covering that allowed him to see a bit of sunlight. I remembered the sparkle in Marija's eyes when she told me how she was allowed to sit outside in the tall cement-walled enclosure one day and a ladybug landed on her finger. She was enraptured by the beauty and life force of the tiny insect.

I came outside this morning to sit by a stream and restore myself. The open space, the sound of water flowing, the sight of shiny wet rocks, the sun warming my shoulders were medicine that lifted me beyond myself and my life situation. I was connected to something greater than me, something that warmed and fed me. I was reminded that I was worthy of breath and this spot on the earth. And that I shared life force with the spinning aspen leaves, the soaring raptors, the taunting mayflies. I was at once expanded and made small in the pattern of life. I was refreshed; my concerns were laid before the range of mountains nearby and brought down to size.

I wanted this for the inmates. I wished they could sit on the banks of this creek and become restored. They needed it more than I did. Swallows dove to catch insects so tiny I couldn't spot them, an American ouzel dipped for its breakfast underwater. A father sauntered nearby with a barefoot little girl in a pink sun hat who toddled behind him, hauling water toys. A young boy raced a leaf he had tossed into the water upstream. He lost the race and tried again with a new leaf.

It might be worth bringing back chain gangs if the goal was not work but rather restoration of the spirit in the natural world. A chance to let nature show how everything passed, how we were all connected, how renewal was everywhere, and liveliness was worth aligning with. I sipped my chilled coffee drink and imagined a chain gang of Teton County inmates sitting on the green grassy bank of Cache Creek alongside me, watching a black crow bathe, the flutter of its feathers sending a spray of jeweled droplets, or following the yellow butterfly swooning over clover, maybe taking off their canvas slippers and wading.

Most of all, I wished the inmates this silence that cupped organic sounds of life: water slipping over rocks, breezes brushing pine needles, a toddler laughing.

# [ Chapter Twenty-Seven ]

I once read about some research done on the power of different kinds of prayer. As I remember it, two flats of seedlings and two groups of people were involved. One group addressed their flat of seedlings with prayers to grow into healthy, tall, leafy plants. The other group prayed for their seedlings to grow to their highest potential, leaving open what that might be.

Whenever I recount this to others and ask which flat they thought became the most robust set of plants, most everyone guesses the first flat. But the research discovered it was the second. I suspect it was because we humans are limited in our imaginations in comparison to the intelligence of the natural energies.

Often, when meeting with the inmates, I found myself getting tense with certain hopes and sometimes sent prayers pleading for an outcome I viewed as best. Please let Kevin be released to his family, who has traveled here from Florida, arriving in single-digit temperatures, in the hope that the judge will release him to be escorted home, rather than sending him to further time in the state prison. Don't let Jeffrey be sentenced to yet more months in the county jail; give him probation instead.

Please let the court send Jack to rehab, and let Curtis realize deep down how worthy he is. On and on.

The tension I felt in my body and mind at such times should have been a clue that I was straining to control a situation I had no control over. And should have reminded me that I carried no real insight and wisdom over how life should go for these men.

When I remembered to, I prayed: May you grow to reach your highest potential. I released each man to himself and his journey. And when I did this, I visibly relaxed. My shoulders dropped, my toes uncurled.

We were all becoming. We were all in the process of reaching our highest potential. What more could we ask than this?

# [ Chapter Twenty-Eight ]

Drew was back in jail. The first time we met, a year ago, he was eighteen. He said then that his wife and the mother of their newborn son had turned him in for using drugs. At that time he was given probation. He broke his probation, returned to jail a second time, and the court once again released him on probation. Tonight was his third incarceration in little over a year.

Oddly, it was always a nice reunion when an inmate returned, a pleasure for me to see their familiar face and some relief too, knowing the guy was still alive. It was pleasant for the returning inmate as well to have someone so happy to see them, despite their difficult circumstances.

Drew said, "I've been clean since you saw me last. Six months now." But he was living in Oregon, not Wyoming, where he was supposed to be living and regularly checking in with his probation officer. Nineteen years old now, he was referring to another woman as his wife and said she might be pregnant.

Drew was tall and thin, with pale-red hair and lightly freckled skin. I picked up a year ago that he was easygoing. And then I picked up that he was *too* easygoing. In fact, that was his

MO, his defended way of meeting life. Drew felt anger toward nobody, despite what they may have done to him. He smiled through his stories of nasty treatment from his sisters. He told how his friends had ripped him off, how his former wife withheld visits with his son.

And he said often about this treatment, "That's okay."

And I replied just as often, "No, it's not okay."

"People need fresh chances," he said tonight about learning that his new wife had turned him in this time. "I don't hold grudges."

After catching up with the men's news, I gave a journaling prompt. Tonight it was to write about a betrayal. Afterward each man read and discussed what he had written. Drew wrote that his buddy had been keeping his car for him during the second sentence he'd served, and when he was released he'd learned that his friend had sold Drew's car for drugs. Accepted $300 for it.

Drew said, "I rebuilt the car myself, every piece of it. It was worth at least three thousand dollars." He added, "But that's okay."

Drew helped me remember how I was still wrestling with the same issues and forgiving the same people, year after year. Decades ago I thought I was doing so because I was a good person. Turning the other cheek and all. Drew thought he was a good person too.

But I suspected that neither Drew nor I had the self-esteem or confidence to stand up for ourselves and say, "No more."

Because what if we did? Things would change. New relationships with others would be required. And Drew and I weren't up to that. So we forgave, stayed with the same people who offered the same treatment, which allowed us to turn that bruised cheek once again and feel wonderful about ourselves: we were so forgiving with our large hearts.

I felt a bit embarrassed about how long I'd taken to catch on. I was five decades older than Drew, and when I looked at him and saw his slight smile while he was telling me about his best friend who sold his car, I was looking at myself.

"Is he still your best friend, Drew?"

"Oh, yeah. I know he didn't mean anything."

That was just what I did in my own mind: I excused the person promptly, convinced they would soon realize what they'd done and feel regretful, and then feel grateful to me for hanging in there with the relationship. Clearly both Drew and I were stalling with this self-image of flawless victim because we didn't want to have to face the truth or deal with it.

Oh, yeah. I know he didn't mean anything.

Drew smiled. It was a genuine smile, sweet.

What was wrong with this picture?

Drew was addicted to drugs of various kinds, and he endured abuse from family, friends, probably strangers. He was smart. In the areas that interested him, he demonstrated persistence. Cars and the computer technology that was involved in repairing them were his areas of expertise. Drew had two sisters, both drug addicts. Neither treated him well. They talked their nice-guy brother into buying drugs for them. They tried to get him to join them in taking drugs. And when he managed to stay clean, they turned on him. Said abusive things and shunned him. This family pattern may be the root of Drew's deep need to please.

But what was mine?

Like Drew, my yearning to please seemingly had no limits.

I had even been guilty of trying to please my dog Emmett by waking him from a nap to alert him to the approach of the garbage truck. Emmett liked to race across the yard, barking in excitement every Thursday afternoon trying to catch the treats the driver tossed from his window. I hated to have him miss that.

The court gave Drew a choice: one more chance to meet his probation, which would last five years this time, and if he messed up he was off to prison. Or he could go straight to prison for two years and be done with the courts.

"I don't see how I can keep from messing up for five years. I'll try, but I know I can't do it."

"So what's going to keep you from just messing up on the first day with that attitude?"

He shrugged. "I don't know. My son, I guess."

Drew had brought me photos of his now sixteen-month-old baby. I pictured that little boy growing up in the situation Drew had painted over the months. "That's a darn good reason to stay out of prison." I said, "Your baby boy needs you, Drew."

There was about as much backbone in Drew's statement with the added "I guess" as there was in mine when I let unmet promises, big and small, from my family or friends go by with yet another promise.

"Please don't toss your red sweatshirt into the washing machine when I'm washing my white clothes. Turns everything pink."

"Yeah, okay. I won't."

"Promise? You've done this before."

"Promise."

The following week: "All the white sheets and towels are pink."

"Oh. Well, my sweatshirt was dirty."

And I let that slide. Said not one word in support of myself. As Drew would say, "Oh, yeah, I know he didn't mean it."

Reciprocity, as another friend and I discussed, was a universal law. That exchange of energy in the form of attention and care held the heart of relationships. But Drew was more comfortable giving than receiving, and maybe the same was true about me.

During the drive home from the jail I was shaking my head over Drew being arrested for the third time in about twelve months, wondering why the guy didn't recognize the repetition of the patterns in his life.

Then this morning I reached for an old journal of mine during breakfast to jot down a thought and discovered, as I leafed through looking for a blank page, that I had described issues years ago that I was still grappling with today. In journal entry after entry, I was wrestling with my resistance to reality. I was jogging in place. Like Drew, I was thinking each time: Oh, yeah, I know he didn't mean it.

May 1999 journal entry: "I have to let go. No more striving for something not within our reach."

Today: Still striving.

August 2012 journal entry: "Expect nothing, hope for nothing. Pay attention to actions, not words."

Today: Still expecting, still hoping, still banking on words.

Never mind Drew, it was me who wasn't paying attention or being responsible for what I experienced.

Some people paid $150 an hour or more to a therapist to work toward personal understanding. I seemed to be accomplishing the same thing for free, meeting with the inmates on Tuesday nights. Over the past seven years I had saved thousands of dollars.

Life had been long for me and treated me with patience. I had the luxury of taking my time to learn about myself. But I worried about the inmates. They didn't have time on their side. Addiction and the threat of long-term imprisonment made repeating their mistakes a grave danger.

# [ Chapter Twenty-Nine ]

Persistence. Does it come from a strong inner force, a reservoir deep with positive energy? Or does it come from an unwillingness to change course? Or perhaps disbelief of my own negative experiences? Wherever it comes from, I seem to have an unending flow of it.

I could make Elizabeth Warren, recipient of the famous line from Senator McConnell, "Nevertheless, she persisted" look like a wimp in the face of how many years I have held course once I embarked on something. My goals were not as lofty as Senator Warren's, and in some cases I persisted because I felt reluctant to move on.

My persistence pushed me through fifteen years of rejections to my writing — novels, short stories, essays, all rejected. And it pushed me through many years of relationships in which I felt only I was fully participating. That made my persistence both my most admirable strength and my biggest weakness.

I have used persistence to show myself the well of love and patience I can carry for another. In relationships that lasted decades. And I had used persistence to absorb damage from others for just as long. I had to ask myself whether I had done so because of that reservoir of love and patience or because I wasn't convinced I deserved better.

Shawn, an inmate I met with recently, said, "I was persistent in my attempts to have a relationship with my mother and grandmother because I needed something from the people in my life." At age eight he had opted for living with a foster family, and yet he continued to feel a need for a loving connection with his mother and grandmother. Once he was old enough he moved back in with them and tried to have a loving family situation. He explained to the group one Tuesday night that he wanted a relationship with his family of origin so much that he joined them in their addiction.

He was now in his early twenties and in jail for having so much meth in the home and car he shared with his girlfriend that their nine-month-old baby was addicted when the two were arrested.

What had I needed so much that I persisted, even when the signals were urging a turn in another direction? What did I need from the people in my life?

I had gotten clear about my writing rejections. I moved through the doubt and landed on the side of continuing to do what made me feel most alive. I learned to detach from the outcome — in this case, rejection — which I realized was none of my business since I had no control over it. I kept writing. I kept feeling more and more alive. And I was improving, educating myself about the craft I loved. There was joy in that.

Was there a clue in there about dealing with family members, friends?

In part I believed that if I kept at the relationships, I'd get better at them too, that in time they'd become reciprocal. I did get better at them, but they didn't all become reciprocal. And ultimately that was the lesson for me. I learned that just as with writing, I needed to let go of the outcomes. They were none of my business. My business was all about learning, deep within, as much about the experience of love as I could. It was really just about me, not about rejection at all. I still loved each of these people, I enjoyed whatever level of exchange they could engage in, I wasn't waiting for anyone to catch on or catch up, at least on my best days. I was in the business of aliveness. I loved whoever accompanied me in that endeavor, no matter how briefly or conditionally. Sometimes that meant my pups, Zoe and Emmett, sometimes family members or friends, sometimes a sensationally beautiful plant at the grocery store, sometimes the sky. I discovered I was never lonely, I rarely felt rejected, and if I did, I could take a step inward and remember some truths like: take nothing personally; everything changes; people try to make you feel the way they feel inside.

We learn life lessons the fastest when suffering is involved, sadly. I needed some suffering to receive the lessons, and Shawn realized the same.

Shawn lost the struggle of persistence to get his mother and grandmother to love and care for him. Once he was arrested, they didn't visit him once for the six months he was in jail, and he was just up the road. My persistence had worked out a bit better for me. I learned I was strong, patient, steady in my heart. And I understood those were the things I was after. I just had confused them with the reflections bounced back from the mirrors I set up for myself that told me about the world and how I fit in it. What was always true was that the inner told us more than the outer. Toward the end of his incarceration, Shawn realized he had gained a lot from his persistence as well. He knew now to go after what really mattered to him, which was not how much others loved him but how much he loved himself.

# [ Chapter Thirty ]

I had hiked up Snow King Mountain behind my house to a place I was calling my office to write outside on this gorgeous July morning. A fallen log a few feet off the path, in the shade of pine trees and surrounded by wildflowers, served as my desk area. The top of the log had been deeply clawed by a bear searching for an insect snack, which created a comfortable dip for my butt. My notebook rested on my knees and other supplies — including bear spray in case she returned — were in my backpack, leaning against the log beside me. I liked eating outside, so I'd brought along lunch. At home there was a snack drawer in my desk, second one down on the left. So I should say that I like to eat anywhere, and especially seem to have a hand-to-mouth deal going when I write.

The flies were pesky this morning, swirling around my head, trying to get in my eyes. It reminded me of when I conducted a writing workshop in Tanzania while on safari and I watched a massive male lion resting in the shade of the Serengeti, appearing serene and content. On closer look I saw dozens of black flies swarming his face. Unlike the lion, who seemed accepting of the pests, I swatted at the flies, sending them off with insults. On the Snow King slopes the wildflowers were plentiful. Shiny purple flax swayed in a light breeze, and the heavy heads of sunflowers nodded. Nearer the ground I spotted harebells and reminded myself to pick a few for my salad tonight. Creating a vibrant contrast in color, the scarlet Indian paintbrush waved in grasses made neon-green from summer rains.

I felt especially leery of moose this morning, swinging my head around at every dropped pinecone. Perhaps it was because my friend, the writer Tim Sandlin, experienced a close call with a fast-running moose that almost crashed into him by the creek below me a couple of days earlier. I knew that particular moose lived on this part of the mountain. I'd encountered her before when hiking, so buried in trees off trail that I didn't know she was there until the tree limbs near me started to mysteriously dip and sway as she nibbled their twigs.

I was still uneasy about moose since my encounter with a mother who'd charged me and knocked me down. But also I felt like a woman touched by wildness in a way I had not been before. Once a spectator, now I felt marked as a player. I knew in the way of atoms, in the way of blurring the definitions between moose and human and grass and creek, that I was a part of it all and that all of it was a part of me. I knew this from the memory held in the ladder of muscles along my back and from the clutch in my throat during the silent intimacy the moose and I later shared when she came to my window.

But sadly, I also knew it in my alertness to the possibility of another surprise encounter, and on some days like today, I became a bit edgy and looked behind me often. Still, nothing thrilled me more than to spot a moose napping in my yard or browsing the wild rosehips, fat as cherries and dosed with vitamin C, beside my house.

Because it was a holiday, the Fourth of July, and peak

tourist season in Jackson Hole, I heard the extra-heavy traffic on Broadway beneath the calls and whistles of birds. Up here the traffic sounded like the shushing of ocean waves topping a pebbled beach. Today was an especially fun holiday for kids, with the western parade planned in town for this morning and the fireworks scheduled for tonight. I tallied up how many children were spending the holiday without the fathers I met with in the jail workshop last night. Fourteen. The youngest was sixteen months old, the oldest sixteen years old.

The father of the youngest was Drew, who opted for a sentence in the state prison instead of that five-year probation he was worried about. His theory was that he would do his time and be done with it rather than having it hang over his head for five years. Drew, with his reddish-blond sweetness, his nice-guy I-can't-say-no smiling face, didn't belong in prison but rather in a finishing school, if there were such a thing for young men raised without guidance or role models. He could use courses in how not to be taken advantage of, how to manage money, how not to believe everything everyone said. And maybe birth control, since he recently confirmed the new wife was indeed pregnant.

Drew professed great love for his son but set up his life to avoid having to deal with the child's mother. Fortunately, Drew's mother enjoyed a consistent relationship with his son and did her best to bridge the gap between her son and grandson. During Drew's past incarcerations he had brought photos of his baby to the workshop regularly, so I felt as if I'd watched the little guy grow from an infant to a toddler.

Last night I said, "Bring in new pictures of Chance when you can, Drew."

"Yeah," Drew said. "I can't believe he's almost two already."

And I thought — because I was still a bit startled to have Drew back here in jail again — yeah, I can't believe you're not with him. My heart sank, realizing that with Drew in prison, the little guy will be without his father for some years to come.

I remembered now that during a workshop a year ago I had asked Drew to write down the name of a person he admired, along with their qualities. He named his uncle, a man he loved and in whose company he'd grown up; he included a good list of his admirable characteristics. And then Drew added, "He's in prison now. I'm not going to be like that, but he's a good guy."

A butterfly big as a warbler just flew past me, close enough to make me yank my head up from my notebook. And now that I looked around, I saw several butterflies of all sizes doing touch-and-go landings on the wild geraniums, pale-pink and chest high, growing beside the path. The air smelled dry and faintly of sun-warmed cinquefoil rose blooms. The bear should consider returning because the log was host to fat brown ants and a pinpoint of a bug with high-end tuxedo markings.

I was celebrating the holiday alone, a deliberate decision. The long weekend had been crowded with people. A hundred and fifty-six, to be exact. The Jackson Hole Writers Conference was scheduled heavily for me with critiquing manuscripts, giving a workshop, signing books, meeting new people, and gathering with old friends. By Sunday evening I was dizzy with the need for solitude and silence. When I spent several days in a row being around people, a lump formed in my throat and a sense of longing occurred, as though I missed myself. And so this morning alone on the mountain.

# [ Chapter Thirty-One ]

Aaron was in his midtwenties, built strongly, with dark hair cut short and blue eyes that didn't seem to miss much. This was the second time he'd been incarcerated here for domestic battery, both times accused by the same woman. The first time Aaron was jailed for a week, released on a Friday, arrested again the following Tuesday. This second time he was put in maximum security. During Aaron's visit down to see me, he was spewing anger. His body shifted restlessly on the plastic chair.

"I've written shit all over the walls of that stupid-ass dinky cell, and I pace from one piece of shit I've penciled at eye level to the next one."

"Hmm," I said, "sounds kind of like walking meditation, except the goal is to feel calm inside rather than fury."

Aaron's body stilled. "What's walking meditation?"

I stood up on my side of the locked-down grated room and showed him how to walk mindfully. Slow steps, attention directed inwardly.

Aaron didn't come down for the following Tuesday-night workshop. When that happened, I tried not to judge myself about having failed to say the right things when I had the chance. But then he came to see me the week after that.

"I erased all the shitty crap I wrote on my walls."

"You did?"

"Yeah. Now I've got four things written, one on each wall. Things like: Stay strong. Be calm. And now I'm doing more like you were saying."

"What's that?"

"I'm doing a walking meditation. I walk from one saying to another over and over." Aaron nodded and smiled. "I'm feeling pretty good."

This is what I find wonderful about understanding there really are no opposites, no one place, for example, where cold becomes hot, but rather a continuum. One step, one degree, on the continuum from what does not work for us to what does. That was how Aaron moved from fury to calm. Two weeks later, when he was released from max and able to join the regular workshop, he was referring to himself as a man in need of help, and he was taking steps to get it.

This is why I continued volunteering at the jail on Tuesday nights. Who else got to witness this kind of uplifting event every week? I watched realization wash across faces, saw insight widen eyes, caught features soften when the men were encouraged to offer self-compassion. What I did was merely nod toward a light switch. The inmates themselves flipped it on.

Joseph Campbell said, "Your sacred space is where you can find yourself again and again."

That made jail Aaron's sacred space.

And mine.

# [ Epilogue ]

As I've mentioned, aside from the journaling workshops, the inmates had no scheduled interaction with the community or opportunities to grow or learn outside a small jail library. Upon request AA sponsors met with individuals, and church services were occasionally held. Otherwise time stretched endlessly for the inmates, with nothing to frame the day but three bland meals and disrupting bed checks.

I had noticed a pattern. The first week an inmate struggled with feeling angry at being arrested and tended to blame others, the police, the town, friends, or family. The second week an inmate struggled with despair and self-blame emerged, swamping them with a sense of failure, shame, guilt, and low self-esteem. By the third week inmates often turned a corner into vows to change and improve their lives. This was when the journaling workshops became of particular interest to them. There was enthusiasm, even excitement, over the idea of change, and inmates began to dream, make plans. But there was no way to begin those dreams, take steps toward those plans. So the dreams and plans circled around their minds over and over until dulled by repetition. And finally, apathy set it.

It was deeply sorrowing to witness this. At last a person

had emerged from their drug- or alcohol-induced numbness to remember themselves, to recall that they were someone with hopes and intentions. Yet there was nowhere to go but back into numbness: sleeping the day away, watching TV for hours.

For seven years I had wanted so much for the inmates. More than I could manage to get for them. I didn't even know where to begin. Rather, I felt as stuck and demoralized as the way the inmates tended to feel over the situation.

Then one day a man named Ben phoned. He'd recently begun volunteering at the jail himself and had heard about my journaling workshops. He had realized the inmates had problems he could solve. For instance, their cars were often parked on public property at their arrest, and soon they would be charged towing costs plus a hefty daily price for storage. Ben found private property to legally park the cars at no cost for the duration of the inmate's incarceration. He accomplished banking errands. He arranged for rent payments or moved belongings, and he found temporary homes for the inmates' pets. Our phone call lasted an hour; we had so much to say to each other. It was satisfying to talk about my experience with someone who understood what I was doing and who shared the challenges I was dealing with. I admired this guy and how he had perceived a need and a way to fulfill it.

Soon after, Ben and I met at a local coffee shop and practically talked on top of each other in our enthusiasm about the improvements we'd like to see happen at the jail. We agreed incarceration needed to be used as more than a punishment. We wanted to offer opportunities for the inmates to come out of jail in a better position than when they went in.

For our next meeting Ben invited his friend Len to join us. Len referred to the inmates as "our incarcerated brothers and sisters," which made me like him right away. Both men had that rare combination of superb intelligence and deeply felt heart energy. With my seven years of experience in the jail, the three of us made a strong team.

Ben created a formal list of the topics we had discussed as needing attention. Then we asked for a meeting with the Teton County sheriff, whose department overlooked the detention center. Sheriff Carr, an intelligent, progressive, humorous man, was fully on board with the ideas we suggested for expanding the experiences of the men and women who were incarcerated.

Laptops for the inmates headed our list. We wanted the inmates to have the ability to take classes, to acquire degrees and certifications for jobs. The following year this goal seemed out of reach. Nevertheless, we inched our way toward it. We applied for grants and gave public talks.

And then one day, when we had earned only a fraction toward the thousands we needed, we received notice of an unimaginably generous donation. Ten spanking-new laptops were going to be delivered to the jail. A local man, who had learned our team was working on getting the funding for laptops and who had helped to educate us about the right product, sent them to the jail. The laptops arrived fully loaded with an expanded library, inspiring TED Talks, classes from the Kahn Academy, and opportunities to acquire degrees and certifications. Our team's gratitude was boundless.

Many of the goals on our team's list involve more interaction between inmates and community members. We believe that if more people come to the jail to offer classes, discussion groups, meditation sessions, and such, inmates might feel less excluded from the community and more likely to become meaningful members once released. Over the years the inmates have expressed an abundance of gratitude that I had chosen to spend time with them in jail when I had many other choices. I like to imagine how they would feel knowing more people from our community made such a decision. Although the detention center is located a few blocks from our town square, most residents are unaware of its presence; I know I was once. Our team intends to break through that strong division between the jail and the community. We believe it will enhance the lives of all of us.

# [ Workbook ]

In March 2020 the pandemic closed the jail to the public. The inmates were allowed no visitors and no journaling workshops. I can't imagine how that multiplied the miserable march of days for the incarcerated men and women. In an effort to offer the inmates a guide toward looking inward and conducting their own inquiries, I created a workbook that simulated our time together in the journaling workshops. My teammates Ben and Len found the funding for producing it. We keep the detention center supplied with the workbooks, and the officers agreed to pass them out.

The workbook consists of fifteen lessons. Each lesson offers five questions and is accompanied by a few of my favorite quotes. I hope the questions and quotes provide readers with new pathways as they engage in their own journeys inward.

*What we bring into the light, we can work with.*
*What remains in the dark, works us.*

Tina Welling

## PART 1

*I wish I could show you*
*when you are lonely or in darkness*
*the astonishing light*
*of your own being.*

Hafiz

1. Write a list of three people you admire and enjoy. They may be living or dead; friends, family, or strangers; real or from books or movies.
2. Now write a list of the characteristics or qualities of each of these people.

   The good news:

   These characteristics and qualities belong to you. You wouldn't recognize them in others if you didn't already own them or have the seeds of those characteristics in yourself.
3. Choose three of the characteristics that you'd like to strengthen within yourself, and write them down.
4. Write about the steps you will take to bring these qualities into your life more fully.
5. Create a short sentence or mantra that reminds you of who you really are at your center. For example: "I am a person who is loving, kind, and generous."

   Memorize this mantra, and repeat it often to keep aware of your intentions.

*You do not become good by trying to be good,*
*but by finding the goodness that is*

*already within you*
*and allowing that goodness to emerge.*

Eckhart Tolle

*I am not what happened to me,*
*I am what I choose to become.*

Carl Jung

# PART 2

*There is nothing in the world, I venture to say, that would so effectively help one to survive even the worst conditions as the knowledge that there is a meaning in one's life.*

Viktor E. Frankel

1. There may be people who have given you acceptance and approval. List the positive things they've said about you. Believe them.
2. Research shows that we feel good about ourselves when we offer help to others. List what you can give to another. As you've experienced, even smiles and kind words are powerful.
3. Name and describe one skill you'd like to learn in order to fulfill yourself and to contribute to your community, and explain why.
4. We feel that life is meaningful when we have something to contribute. So when you think of your interests, skills, gifts, and passions, what would you enjoy offering to others? Write about this idea.

*You cannot get through a single day without having an impact on the world around you. What you do makes a difference, and you have to decide what kind of difference you want to make.*

Jane Goodall

5. List ways you can be your own best friend and ways you can act as a loving parent to yourself, starting right now, right here.

*If you make friends with yourself you'll never be alone.*

Maxwell Maltz

## PART 3

*Talk to yourself like you would to someone you love.*

Brené Brown

*If we shame ourselves, we believe we end up loving ourselves. It has never been true, not for a moment, that shame leads to love. Only love leads to love.*

Geneen Roth

*So why is self-compassion a more effective motivation than self-criticism? Because its driving force is love, not fear.*

Kristen Neff

1. Imagine yourself as a small child. List what you love about the child you were. Know that you hold all the

sweetness, goodness, and lovability of this child at your core.

2. Claim everything about yourself, the good, the bad, the ugly, and the beautiful. Start with your body and then move on to your actions, your choices, your history. Along the way, acknowledge your emotions and claim those too. Own all the parts of your life, and find peace with your story.
3. Caring for the things and the living beings around you enhances a sense of belonging to Life. Name some actions you can take right now to create a stronger bond with the aliveness around you.
4. What do you find yourself waiting for? There is only now, so take steps toward this goal at once, in every way you can imagine. Look within. Everything you need is there.
5. You breathe, you are a living force on Earth. Life is a sacred responsibility. How can you care for yourself right now to honor this idea?

*The privilege of a lifetime is being who you are.*

Joseph Campbell

## PART 4

*Self-awareness is the ability to take an honest look at your life without attachment to it being right or wrong.*

Debbie Ford

*Knowing yourself is the beginning of all wisdom.*

ARISTOTLE

*Go back and take care of yourself. Your body needs you,*
*your feelings need you, your perceptions need you.*
*Your suffering needs you to acknowledge it. Go home*
*[to yourself] and be there for all these things.*

THICH NHAT HANH

1. How does your body feel lately?
   What does it need more of?
   What does it need less of?
2. What kind of emotions have you had today? This week?
3. What is on your mind? What concerns you, worries you, lifts your mood or weighs it down?

*I understood myself only after I destroyed myself. And only in the process of fixing myself, did I know who I really was.*

SADE ANDRIA ZABALA

4. What kind of company have you been for yourself? Can you soothe yourself, be understanding of your miserable moods, find your contentment? What kindnesses have you done for yourself lately?
5. In what ways have you abandoned yourself, not acted on your true feelings, or not protected yourself from hurtful behavior from yourself or others?

# PART 5

*Self-awareness involves deep personal honesty.*
*It comes from asking and answering hard questions.*

Stephen Covey

*The wound is the place where the light enters you.*

Rumi

1. When did you know you were strong enough to withstand pain, betrayal, disappointment, and whatever else life might present to you?
2. It is said by many wisdom teachers that every problem holds a gift, and you have the problem because you need the gift. Viewing life this way helps us move from being a victim to being a survivor. What gifts have the difficulties in your life offered you?
3. Are you holding on to something or someone you need to let go of? Write about that.
4. What questions are you asking yourself or your higher heart/mind right now? Write the question and the thoughts that come with it. You may not receive a solution immediately, but you will always receive further information.
5. What is important enough to you that you feel willing to fail over and over again in your attempts to succeed?

*The secret of life is to fall seven times and to get up eight times.*

Paulo Coelho

*If you have never failed, you have never tried.*

SHENG-YEN

## PART 6

Circle all the qualities in the list below that describe you. Write about how these qualities have served you. Make an additional list of the qualities you'd like to strengthen or bring into your life.

| | | |
|---|---|---|
| Accepting | Courageous | Friendly |
| Active | Courteous | Fulfilled |
| Adventurous | Creative | Fun-loving |
| Ambitious | Curious | Funny |
| Approachable | Decisive | Generous |
| Articulate | Dedicated | Gentle |
| Artistic | Dependable | Genuine |
| Assertive | Determined | Good listener |
| Bold | Diplomatic | Good-natured |
| Brave | Direct | Grateful |
| Calm | Disciplined | Grounded |
| Carefree | Down-to-earth | Happy |
| Caring | Easygoing | Hardworking |
| Cautious | Empathic | Helpful |
| Centered | Energetic | Honest |
| Cheerful | Enthusiastic | Hopeful |
| Committed | Ethical | Humble |
| Compassionate | Expressive | Imaginative |
| Confident | Fair-minded | Independent |

| | | |
|---|---|---|
| Conscientious | Faithful | Industrious |
| Considerate | Firm | Insightful |
| Content | Flexible | Intelligent |
| Cooperative | Focused | Intuitive |
| Inventive | Perceptive | Self-confident |
| Kind | Persistent | Self-controlled |
| Knowledgeable | Personable | Self-reliant |
| Likable | Polite | Sensitive |
| Logical | Positive | Sincere |
| Loving | Practical | Strong |
| Loyal | Principled | Supportive |
| Mature | Productive | Tender |
| Modest | Realistic | Thoughtful |
| Motivated | Reflective | Tolerant |
| Observant | Relaxed | Trusting |
| Optimistic | Reliable | Understanding |
| Orderly | Resilient | Warm |
| Organized | Resourceful | Worthy |
| Patient | Respectful | |
| Peaceful | Responsible | |

## PART 7

*People say that what we're all seeking is a meaning for life. I don't think that's what we're really seeking. I think that what we're seeking is an experience of being alive... so that we actually feel the rapture of being alive.*

Joseph Campbell

1. Self-judgments are painful. Research shows that feelings of shame often are linked to substance or behavior addictions. Both shame and addiction prevent a sense of full aliveness. So begin to acknowledge the negative judgments you carry about yourself by writing about them here.
2. Offer yourself understanding. Not excuses, but a deeply caring attempt to understand the roots of any regrets you carry.
3. Chances are you did your best at the time of any regretful actions. Perhaps you saw few or no choices. Perhaps you were trying to survive in a hard world. Write about that.
4. Harsh self-talk puts limits on our personal growth. So be your own good supporter and write positive statements about your ability to make good choices.
5. Self-forgiveness is liberating. It takes practice. Begin by writing about how good it will feel to accept yourself and move onward in your life.

*It is time to set yourself free — and in doing so,*
*you will free others as well.*

ELIZABETH GILBERT

*I decided the most subversive, revolutionary thing I could do*
*was to show up for my life and not be ashamed.*

ANNE LAMOTT

## PART 8

*Forgive others, not because they deserve forgiveness,*
*but because you deserve peace.*

Jonathan Lockwood Huie

1. Consider a person who has harmed you. What do you imagine caused them to act that way?
2. People try to make others feel the way they feel. Describe how you felt when harmed emotionally. Consider whether the person who harmed you felt similar emotions caused by someone else in their life.

*I will permit no man to narrow and degrade my soul*
*by making me hate him.*

Booker T. Washington

*A child that's being abused by its parents doesn't stop*
*loving its parents, it stops loving itself.*

Shahida Arabi

3. When people are harmed by others, often they repeat the harm unconsciously to themselves. In what ways have you harmed yourself?
4. Forgiveness takes practice. The first step in freeing ourselves from the bondage of refusing to forgive is to claim: "I am willing to begin the process of forgiveness." Write this line repeatedly, filling in the necessary name or your own.

*The definition of mercy is undeserved forgiveness.*

John Travis

5. Forgiveness doesn't mean carrying on with the person who hurt you as if the harm didn't happen; it means carrying on with your life without the burden of their actions. Write about how that might work for you.

## PART 9

*Gratitude unlocks the fullness of life.*
*It turns what we have into enough, and more.*

Melody Beattie

1. If you can acknowledge that your painful experiences also gave you something you're grateful for, such as strength, it transfers power from the offender to the victim. Write a letter of gratitude to a difficult person.

*Buddhist logic says that if you plant a lemon seed and pray for a mango fruit, logically it won't work. But this is what we do; wish for happiness without planting the seeds of happiness.*

Khandro Rinpoche

2. Plant seeds of happiness with the awareness of gratitude by writing an ongoing list of what you appreciate about your life.

*Cultivate the habit of being grateful for every good thing that comes to you, and to give thanks continuously.*

*And because all things have contributed to your advancement, you should include all things in your gratitude.*

Ralph Waldo Emerson

3. Gratitude is the opposite of complaint. List your complaints, and find their opposites in gratitudes. Practice holding both in your awareness.

*Studies show that grateful individuals tend to feel more happy, hopeful, vital, and satisfied with their lives.*

Kristin Neff

4. Research shows that gratitude can be learned. Create a practice by choosing a time of day when you will devote a few minutes to feeling grateful.
5. Appreciate yourself. Your entire body pulses with life. Write your appreciation for a part of your body, for example, your hands, eyes, or feet.

*Happiness does not consist in things themselves but in the relish we have of them.*

François de la Rochefoucauld

## PART 10

*The most difficult times for many of us are the ones we give ourselves.*

Pema Chödrön

1. When is it hardest for you to say no? And to whom?

*We cannot simultaneously set a boundary*
*and take care of another person's feelings.*

Melody Beattie

2. Whose emotions do you feel responsible for, and try to take care of or protect, while also trying to maintain your own boundaries and independence?
3. Who in your life pushes you to act in ways not in your best interest? How can you set limits on their influence?
4. List the things you feel you should do or be. Next put an *E* beside those that feel good emotionally, a *B* beside those that feel good to your body, and an *M* beside those that interest your mind. This organizes the "shoulds" and allows you to rethink what may or may not contribute to your life.

*Self-love is essential. Until you learn how to feel loved in an empty room, you will not feel loved for very long in any other room.*

Vironika Tugaleva

5. What do you find yourself doing to be loved? And whose love do you work at trying to get?

*You're only overlooked, rejected, and ignored*
*by the people not meant to be in your life.*
*Let go in peace. Look ahead in gratitude.*

THEMINDSJOURNAL.COM

## PART II

*Resentment is like drinking poison*
*and then hoping it will kill your enemy.*

NELSON MANDELA

1. Resentments can occur when relationships are out of balance. For example, when you give much more than you receive, you are likely to feel resentment toward the person you're giving to. Or if you receive much more than you give, the giver might resent you. Write about how you could adjust the balance in your relationships.

*Strong people don't put others down. They lift them up.*

MICHAEL P. WATSON

2. People try to make you feel the way they feel. When someone belittles you, for instance, though it may not seem that way, they are feeling inadequate. How might this insight be helpful in your relationships?

*Don't take anything personally. What others say and do*
*is a projection of their own reality.*

DON MIGUEL RUIZ

3. The words and actions of others say something about them, not you. Write about the difficult people in your life and how not to take their behavior personally.

4. When do you feel the most frustrated? What about those times makes you feel that way?
5. Resentments can turn into full-blown anger if not addressed. Address them now. In what situations do you feel taken advantage of? Who do you hold a grudge against?

*The struggle you're in today is developing the strength you need for tomorrow. Don't give up.*

ROBERT TEW

## PART 12

*Any person capable of angering you becomes your master; he can anger you only when you permit yourself to be disturbed by him.*

EPICTETUS

1. Your body gives you signals that alert you to your anger. For example: heat, shaking, tightness, numbness. What do you feel in your body when you're angry?
2. What goes on in your mind when you are angry? Blanking out, confusion, a desire to lash out or harm? Describe it to yourself.

*People are afraid that if they let go of their anger… and look at their own feelings — and even see the good in a bad person — they're going to lose the energy they need to do something about the problem. But actually you get more strength and energy.*

ROBERT THURMAN

*Holding on to anger is like grasping*
*a hot coal with the intent of throwing*
*it at someone else; you are the one*
*who gets burned.*

The Buddha

3. What is your first reaction when you feel angry?
4. If the goal is to slow down your first reaction, what helps you do that? Noticing your breath or body sensations, recalling your true self, counting, redirecting your attention, exercising, walking away, talking to someone?

*Let go or be dragged.*

Zen proverb

5. Make a plan for situations that trigger your anger. Create three simple steps for noticing it, slowing it down, dealing with it.

*We repeat what we don't repair.*

Christine Langley-Obaugh

## PART 13

*Personal power is the ability to stand on your own two feet with a smile on your face in the middle of a universe that contains a million ways to crush you.*

J. Z. Colby

1. What is one of the most difficult choices you've had to make?
2. What lesson has taken you the longest to learn?
3. Name some of the best choices you've made so far.

*The one thing you can't take away from me is the way I choose to respond to what you do to me. The last of one's freedoms is to choose one's attitude in any given circumstance.*

Viktor Frankl

*You may not control all the events that happen to you, but you can decide not to be reduced by them.*

Maya Angelou

4. What do you fear most right now?
5. Which of your inner qualities can give you the power to meet those fears?

*For a seed to achieve its greatest expression, it must come completely undone. The shell cracks, its insides come out, and everything changes. To someone who doesn't understand growth, it would look like complete destruction.*

Cynthia Occelli

## PART 14

*What lies behind us and what lies before us are tiny matters compared to what lies within us.*

Ralph Waldo Emerson

1. It is challenging to be true to our inner selves. Name a few things you find difficult about that, for example, other people's opinions, the loneliness of being different, being honest with yourself.

*Be at least as interested in what goes on inside you as what happens outside.*

Eckhart Tolle

*If you get the inside right, the outside will fall into place.*

Eckhart Tolle

2. The author C.S. Lewis tells us we can't change the beginning but we can change the ending. If you started now, how could you create the ending for the situation you find yourself in, whatever that is?

*If you keep going in the same direction,*
*you'll end up in the place you're headed.*

Lao Tze

3. Who do you know who has changed their lives in a boldly positive way? How did they do it? How could you do it?
4. It takes courage to ask for what you need and to reach out for support. Who would you turn to, and what would you ask? Write about what stops you from doing that.
5. Is it more difficult for you to receive love or to give love? Write about that.

## PART 15

*Whatever you can do, or dream you can, begin it.*
*Boldness has genius, power, and magic in it.*

ATTRIBUTED TO JOHANN VON GOETHE

1. Name a goal. Make it specific. Write a few details about it.
2. List the strengths you possess that will help you reach your goal.
3. List any weaknesses to be aware of that perhaps have stopped you before.

*When you are full of problems, there is no room for anything new to enter, no room for a solution. So whenever you can, make room, create some space, so that you find the life underneath your life situation.*

ECKHART TOLLE

4. Name your worries. Which ones can you do something about right now? Which situations can you accept if no change is possible? Which worries can you release to the care of life itself?
5. How will you maintain your enthusiasm during the rough patches?

*From the moment you came into the world*
*a ladder was placed in front of you*
*that you might transcend it.*

RUMI

# [ Acknowledgments ]

This book felt in harmony with my life's rhythms from the start. Pinning language to my experiences with the inmates allowed me to become conscious of my intentions and to gauge my development toward them. That's quite a gift in itself. Then Jason Gardner, executive editor of New World Library, enhanced the experience with his insight and perception, and the gift doubled. Next Tracy Cunningham created a beautiful cover for *Tuesdays in Jail.* Copyeditor Mimi Kusch screened the manuscript with skill and care. Publicist Monique Muhlenkamp guided the book into readers' hands. A heart full of gratitude goes to each of them, along with managing editor Kristen Cashman and all the good people who work at New World Library.

For four years I read aloud chapters of *Tuesdays in Jail* to the Artists & Writers group in Jackson Hole. My fellow members cheered me on month after month as I tested new material. I thank every one of them, beginning with our leaders, Amy Unfried and Anne Muller. My gratitude to members Jean Barash, Alison Brush, Sally Byrne, Sue Cedarholm, Tammy Christel, Betsy Hesser, Nancy Hoffman, Jean Jorgensen, Stephen Lottridge, Susan Marsh, Dee Parker, LeeLee Robert, Chuck

Schneebeck, Betty Walton, and Joy Watson. My friend Janet Hubbard read and critiqued the completed manuscript. The Wyoming Arts Council awarded a creative writing fellowship to an excerpt from *Tuesdays in Jail.*

Lieutenant Troy Sutton of the Teton County Detention Center said yes when I presented my idea of a journaling workshop with the inmates and has supported my Tuesday nights in jail for the past ten years. I thank Sheriff Matt Carr and all the officers of the detention center for the extra work they do to make the workshops happen each week.

Finally, I thank the couple of thousand inmates I've met with so far for sharing their struggles with me and guiding me through mine.

# [ About the Author ]

Tina Welling is the author of *Writing Wild: Forming a Creative Partnership with Nature*, published by New World Library. Her three novels were published by Penguin Random House. Welling's essays have been published in the *New York Times* and in national magazines, as well as in seven anthologies. She can be contacted through her website: www.tinawelling.com.

**NEW WORLD LIBRARY** is dedicated to publishing books and other media that inspire and challenge us to improve the quality of our lives and the world.

We are a socially and environmentally aware company. We recognize that we have an ethical responsibility to our readers, our authors, our staff members, and our planet.

We serve our readers by creating the finest publications possible on personal growth, creativity, spirituality, wellness, and other areas of emerging importance. We serve our authors by working with them to produce and promote quality books that reach a wide audience. We serve New World Library employees with generous benefits, significant profit sharing, and constant encouragement to pursue their most expansive dreams.

Whenever possible, we print our books with soy-based ink on 100 percent postconsumer-waste recycled paper. We power our offices with solar energy and contribute to nonprofit organizations working to make the world a better place for us all.

Our products are available wherever books are sold. Visit our website to download our catalog, subscribe to our e-newsletter, read our blog, and link to authors' websites, videos, and podcasts.

customerservice@newworldlibrary.com
Phone: 415-884-2100 or 800-972-6657
Orders: Ext. 110 • Catalog requests: Ext. 110
Fax: 415-884-2199

**www.newworldlibrary.com**